# A FIGHTING CHANCE
## IN 40 DAYS

# ROSARIO PICARDO

# A FIGHTING CHANCE
## IN 40 DAYS

## 12 STEPS
### TO A NEW LIFE
### IN JESUS

**invite PRESS**

Plano, Texas

*To my amazing wife, Callie, who pushes me toward continuous growth; my three little women of God; and the fantastic congregation of Mosaic Church and Fighting Chance Recovery. Without any of you, this would not have been possible.*

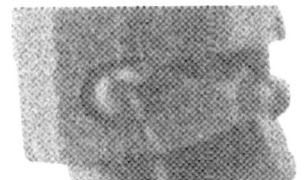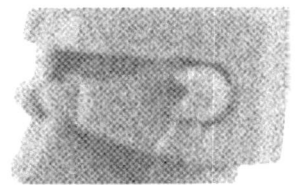

# CONTENTS

# Contents

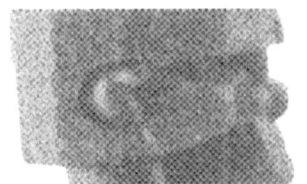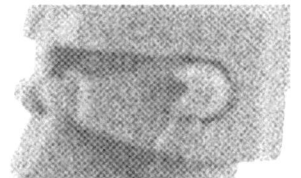

# FOREWORD BY
# MICHAEL ADAM BECK

Frequently in our worship services, we prompt our community in the following way… "Raise your hand if you're in recovery." We continue that prompt until every hand in the room is raised.

Indeed, our church, St. Marks in Ocala, Florida, is home to a holistic recovery housing program called Open Arms Village. Men live, sleep, eat, and shower in the same facility where church folks worship, pray, have meetings, and study scripture. Hundreds of people in recovery gather on our campus each week for daily 12 step meetings. Our team has also cultivated little healing communities in burrito joints, tattoo parlors, and an inpatient substance abuse rehab.

But that hand-raising prompt is not just for "those people." It's also for those we call "normies" too. It turns out that *every person* is in recovery for something. Every single human was formed in *original goodness* and is now healing from *original trauma*, journeying back to *original unity*… the oneness we already are. Maybe my experience looked like an allergic reaction to drugs and alcohol that made me break out in handcuffs and orange jumpsuits, but yours might be over-shopping, judgmentalism, workaholism, negative mental attitudes, or another unhealed trauma.

A biblical theology of recovery is rooted in the transformative understanding of prevenient grace, the idea that God's grace goes before us, seeking us out long before we respond or reciprocate. Recovery is not simply about overcoming struggles but about entering into a journey initiated and sustained by God's love, a love that calls humanity into relationship, healing, and wholeness. Recovery and healing are a response to this divine pursuit, one that requires surrender, trust, and self-examination.

The 12 Steps are not secular but sacred practices deeply rooted in Christian spirituality and the journey of discipleship. They offer a practical, step-by-step "design for living" that mirrors the life of Jesus, inviting participants into humility, surrender, and reconciliation as we cooperate with God's one-day-at-a-time dose of graceful presence. Recovery, therefore, is a lifelong journey of abiding in Christ, surrendering weaknesses to His power, and extending healing grace to others through service and shared witness. It's a life of painting with ashes, using our own still healing wounds like paint brushes. We color this very good world with beauty, truth, and healing on the canvas of each twenty-four hours we are given.

As a person in long-term recovery who has been cultivating fresh expressions of recovery for almost twenty years, it is with deep joy and gratitude that I write this foreword for *A Fighting Chance in 40 Days: 12 Steps to a New Life in Jesus* by my dear friend, Rosario Picardo. Roz is not merely a gifted author and pastor—he is a trusted guide, a voice of compassion, and a seasoned leader whose ministry flows from his own journey of recovery and restoration. This book is a testament to his heart, his faith, and his passion for helping others experience wholeness through the grace of God.

Rosario has done something remarkable here. While the principles of the 12 Steps have historically been associated with recovery from addiction, *A Fighting Chance* demonstrates that these steps are not merely for a specific subset of individuals but for *anyone* seeking a fresh start, deeper connection with God, and personal transformation. They are not just a pathway out of struggle. They are a pathway into God's abundant life, marked by surrender, trust, healing, and hope.

I've seen firsthand the way Rosario weaves theology and recovery into a simple, actionable path for spiritual growth. His personal experience with recovery and his pastoral wisdom both give this book credibility, depth, and practicality. *A Fighting Chance* is not a theoretical exercise. It is a structured journey rooted in scripture, grounded in experience, and designed to lead readers into the transfiguring presence of Jesus Christ. In just 40 days, you will embark on a journey that has the potential to change your heart, renew your mind, and set you on a new trajectory of freedom and peace.

What makes this journey so powerful is that it acknowledges the reality of struggle but refuses to leave readers stuck in it. It offers a hopeful and practical invitation to take the first step, to trust Jesus, and to rely on His strength to lead the way. Each day provides both challenge and encouragement, a roadmap to self-examination, repentance, and renewal—all without shame or condemnation, always with the gentle invitation of grace.

I can think of no better companion on this journey than Rosario Picardo. His honesty about his own journey, combined with his pastoral insights and theological depth, makes this book both accessible and profound. Whether you are new to recovery, new to faith, or simply ready to take an intentional step toward personal and spiritual growth, *A Fighting Chance* offers a pathway to healing and wholeness.

As you embark on this 40-day journey, know that you are not alone. God walks with you every step of the way and so does this guide, designed with prayerful care, wisdom, and love. May you find not just recovery but a restored and vibrant life—a life that reflects the redemptive power of Jesus Christ.

Roz, thank you for your faithfulness, your courage, and your willingness to share this journey with the world. It is my prayer that this book will reach countless individuals in need of hope and healing. May it serve as both a light on the path and an invitation to the kind of transfiguration that only God can bring.

To all who read these pages–take the first step. Begin this journey with faith, knowing that a fighting chance is within your reach.

**MICHAEL ADAM BECK**

Pastor, Professor, Sociologist, Author of *Painting with Ashes* and *Never Alone: Sharing the Gift of Community in a Lonely World.*

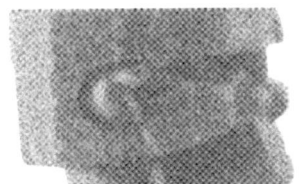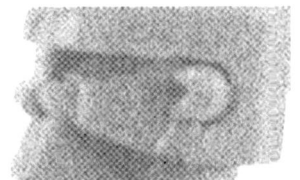

# AN INVITATION TO A JOURNEY

Many people struggle to believe that true transformation is possible. The goal of this study is to give you both the hope that change can really happen and to equip you with a way to experience it.

When you embark on a journey of self-exploration and spiritual growth, you open the door to profound change—change that significantly alters your life and shapes you into a new creation in Jesus. This isn't just self-help or behavior modification; it's a transformation that touches every aspect of your life. When you invite God into the navigator's seat, the Holy Spirit will transform your life into something more abundant, purposeful, and fulfilling than you ever imagined.

*A Fighting Chance in 40 Days: 12 Steps to a New Life in Jesus* guides you through a methodically planned and actionable 40-day journey to uncover the deep insights you need to lead you to healing and wholeness. While the 12 Steps have their roots in addiction recovery, their principles are a pathway for anyone seeking to grow closer to God and embrace the new life Jesus offers. Each step will help you sow the seed of becoming the person God desires for you. This life is better than you could ever have envisioned: one full of power, purpose, and perseverance.

This guide is organized to take you deeper every day. Each day includes a guiding scripture, reflective questions, and practical activities, all designed to help you apply the principles of each step to your life. Each of the 12 Steps spans three days and culminates in a practical activity linked to that step. These steps are not just a roadmap to recovery but a pathway to the new creation God desires for you.

Drawing from my own experience as a pastor who has wrestled with depression and alcoholism, I know firsthand the power of these steps to transform lives. Whether you're confronting personal battles, navigating a season of uncertainty, or simply seeking a closer relationship with Jesus, this journey is for you. It is designed to resonate with all seekers, no matter your background or circumstances. No one is immune from the need for a recovery deliverance or a fresh start, and neither should anyone attempt to walk this path alone. Even "well-known and successful" pastors with huge name recognition like Max Lucado have their own recovery journeys and stories that come with community. This journey is for anyone who is seeking healing and wholeness from "every weight that slows us down, especially the sin that so easily trips us up" (Heb. 12:1 NLT).[1]

This 40-day exploration is not meant to be walked alone. It is best experienced in the company of others—whether with a mentor, a spiritual guide, or a small group. Together, we'll explore themes like self-surrender, acknowledging

---

1.    Max Lucado discusses his personal struggles and restoration by his church elders in Chapter 8 of his book, "*God Never Gives Up on You.*" (Thomas Nelson, 2023)

flaws, making amends, and renewal, each step leading closer to the freedom and wholeness Jesus offers, a life marked by authenticity, responsibility, and grace.

As you begin this journey, remember: every single day is an opportunity for God to do something new in you. Each step forward brings you closer to the unwavering love and abundant life God promises. Let's take this journey together, with receptive hearts and minds, ready to embrace the transformation that comes from becoming a new creation in Christ.

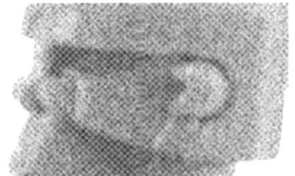

# DAY 1: ORIGIN OF
# THE 12 STEPS

*Therefore, if anyone is in Christ, he is a new creation. The old has passed away; behold, the new has come.*
*– 2 Corinthians 5:17 ESV*

## REFLECTION

As we embark on this 40-day journey, we want to first understand the roots of the 12 Steps. These roots can be traced back to Alcoholics Anonymous (AA) founders Bill Wilson and Dr. Bob Smith. These two remarkable men combined profound spiritual wisdom gained from their own experiences with principles on how our mental and spiritual lives interact with each other as one.

In 1935, Wilson and Smith were each battling alcoholism when they encountered the Oxford Group. This Christian-oriented movement stressed principles such as confession, amends-making, prayer, and living in peace with guidance from God as the foundation for transformation. This encounter had a significant influence on them and paved the path for what is now known as Alcoholics Anonymous

(AA). The core of AA's belief system resides within these 12 Steps, encompassing acknowledgment of wrongs, redemption, and individual growth.

Essentially, the 12 Steps offer a blueprint for overcoming addiction and related struggles, including personal obstacles. Although founded on biblical values, it is crucial to highlight that these steps are adaptable enough to resonate with individuals from diverse religious backgrounds or even those without any religious affiliations. The widespread acceptance and effectiveness of the 12 Steps can be credited to their universal applicability.

Beyond addressing addiction, the 12 Steps provide a multifaceted framework for growth and spiritual development. They allow individuals to reflect inwardly—recognizing their imperfections, seeking forgiveness, and striving for radical change. These acts of introspection, confession, and commitment to change resonate with most religious and spiritual teachings.

The story of Wilson and Smith serves as a testament to the strength found in faith, hope, and community. Their journey from despair to recovery to pioneering an organization that has positively impacted millions of people showcases the power of the 12 Steps. It emphasizes that change is possible, redemption is achievable, and a fulfilling new life is attainable through faith and perseverance.

As we delve into the origins and significance of the 12 Steps, let us always remember their core message: transformation and redemption are within the reach of everyone, regardless of their backgrounds or beliefs. This journey offers hope to all who embark upon it.

# DOING THE INNER WORK

If you are really honest, what change do you long to see in your own heart and life?

Where in your life do you need a new beginning? What would a fresh start look like?

# PRAYER FOCUS

Father, we humbly seek Your guidance as we explore the origins of the 12 Steps. May we gain an understanding of how these principles conform to Your teachings, and may they serve as inspiration for our growth. Please grant us the strength to embrace change and transformation just as You brought renewal to Bill Wilson and Dr. Bob Smith through Your grace and mercy. Amen.

> *Faith has to work twenty-four hours a day in and through us, or we perish. – Bill Wilson*

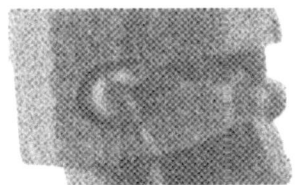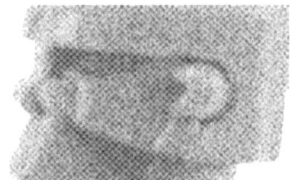

# DAY 2: WALKING IN CHRIST'S FOOTSTEPS THROUGH THE 12 STEPS

*I can do all things through Christ who strengthens me.*
*– Philippians 4:13 NKJV*

## REFLECTION

The 12 Steps in this field guide are not a one-time, one-and-done journey but rather a profound pilgrimage that continues throughout life. Each step is related to the problem of sin, and the solution is following the way of Jesus, the ultimate Higher Power. Through twenty years of pastoral ministry experience, walking alongside many who were battling substance abuse, I've realized something profound: we share common ground as human beings even with "those people" because, essentially, we are the very individuals Jesus sought to rescue.

Engaging in the steps isn't just a program; it's an adventure where countless have found true freedom. As you read through these summaries of the 12 Steps, pause in between and reflect on how they can apply to your own life:

1.  Admit powerlessness
2.  Embrace trust
3.  Find strength in surrender
4.  Embrace self-reflection
5.  Admit our wrongdoings
6.  Confront our flaws
7.  Pursue wisdom
8.  Seek peace
9.  Make amends
10. Embrace daily reflection
11. Seek God's will daily
12. Share changes[1]

The 12 Steps—originally designed to help individuals overcome addiction—offer us a framework for this journey. These steps serve as our guide to recognizing our vulnerabilities and seeking wisdom and guidance from God. They encourage us to reflect on ourselves and acknowledge our mistakes so that we can make amends. They lead us in the practices of confession, repentance, and reconciliation. They motivate us to extend ourselves to the service of others, embodying the teachings of love and compassion exemplified by Christ. By incorporating the principles of the 12 Steps into our lives, we embark on a path that leads to healing and redemption while strengthening our relationship with Christ. This transformative journey enables us to experience God's grace deeply by turning our weaknesses into

---

1.      The summaries represented by these 12 Steps are adapted from *Alcoholics Anonymous,* Alcoholics Anonymous: The Story of How Many Thousands of Men and Women Have Recovered from Alcoholism, 4th ed. (New York: Alcoholics Anonymous World Services, 2001), 59-60.

strengths and transforming our trials into inspiring stories of faith.

## DOING THE INNER WORK

What impediments or difficulties in your life would you like to heal using the 12 Step Program?

Which steps seem like they would be the most challenging for you? Why?

# PRAYER FOCUS

Lord, please be with me as I embark on my journey through the teachings of the 12 Steps. Help me to embrace my insecurities and seek Your guidance. Grant me the strength to acknowledge my mistakes and the humility to ask for forgiveness. As I strive to make amends, let Your spirit of reconciliation guide my actions.

Lead me to demonstrate compassion and selflessness toward others just as Christ taught us. May each step I take serve as a testament to Your grace, turning my weaknesses into strengths and transforming my challenges into ways of bringing You glory and honor. Amen.

> *Hardships often prepare ordinary people for an extraordinary destiny. – C.S. Lewis*

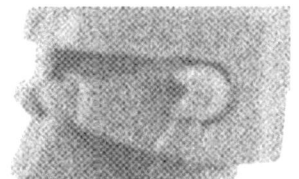

# DAY 3: THE 12 STEPS FOR EVERYONE

> *... for all have sinned and fall short of the glory of God.*
> *– Romans 3:23*

## REFLECTION

In our world, we can encounter divisive people, institutions, and systems that can separate us by highlighting our differences as human beings. When we keep comparing ourselves to others, we create a hierarchy. We either compare ourselves with those we believe are further ahead of us in life—putting ourselves down—or we try to make ourselves feel more important by naming how we are better than those we feel are beneath us.

However, as humans, one of the things that we all have in common is the problem of sin. We live in a fallen world. Sin entered the world long ago in the Garden of Eden with Adam and Eve. Humanity's image has been tainted by sin ever since. We were born into a world marred by original sin. Our bodies, imperfect vessels, fail us. We grapple with an intricate gift from God—our free will—in a world that's off kilter. Romans 3:23 tells us that "all have sinned and fall short of the glory of God." All means all.

Sin includes anything that separates us from God, others, and our own identities. Sin is simply missing the mark—as implied by the Greek word *hamartia*—and we do so in thought, word, deed, and what we purposely leave undone.[1] Sin manifests itself in many ways, and no one can claim to be without sin (Romans 3:23). But the one thing that unites us more incredibly than our sin is that Jesus was born, lived, died, and was resurrected to conquer sin, hell, death, and the grave for *all* people. Jesus' followers specifically seek to break the pattern and cycle of sin because sin is addictive. But Jesus is greater than any addiction.

Often, we consider addiction to be an outward struggle. We think of alcoholics, sex addicts, and those addicted to drugs. Yet, sin also involves the internal things we all struggle with. These internal sins can be deadly to our spirit and equally addictive—sins such as pride, envy, gossip, slander, gluttony, sloth, greed, apathy, selfishness, judgmentalism, and hypocrisy. If we are honest, most of us are prone to one or many of those sins. Our inward and outward problems with sin are manifestations of what is really in our hearts: this is what Jesus came to heal.

The 12 Steps are a vital tool derived from scripture that can help break the addictive power of sin—and, yes, the 12 Steps are for everyone! Notice, I said "a tool." Jesus is the One who saves us, and the 12 Steps point us to Him.

---

1.     Here, when we mention "thoughts," we're specifically addressing the thoughts we create consciously. These are different from uncontrolled or intrusive thoughts often linked to OCD or other psychiatric disorders. This distinction is crucial because many become anxious about their involuntary thought process; yet it's important to recognize that such thoughts aren't inherently sinful.

The 12 Steps were developed both to help people overcome addiction and to provide insights for everyone on the journey of growth and transformation. When viewed from a spiritual perspective, these steps are in line with the teachings of Jesus in emphasizing the renewing of our minds, acknowledging our imperfections, seeking forgiveness, and serving others. They encourage us to embark on a path of self-reflection and change that mirrors the path Jesus walked—one marked by love, forgiveness, and service. Embracing these steps entails committing to our personal growth and readily becoming vessels of God's healing in the world. By doing this, we can deeply experience God's grace while transforming our weaknesses into strengths and turning our trials into stories of faith.

# DOING THE INNER WORK

Recovery requires brave, honest reflection. As you open up to being honest with yourself and God, what sins do you struggle with most?

Knowing you are not alone in struggling with these sins and that Jesus came to set you free, what is your honest request of God? What do you want Jesus to do with these sins you have just named and confessed?

# PRAYER FOCUS

God, I am grateful for the wisdom in the 12 Steps and how they relate to different areas of my life. As I work toward incorporating these principles in my life, please guide me in embodying the teachings of Jesus through my actions. May I be a vessel of Your love, providing peace and service to others and sharing Your message of hope and kindness. In Jesus' name, Amen.

> *I know God won't give me anything I can't handle. I just wish He didn't trust me so much.*
> *– Mother Teresa*

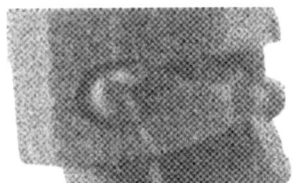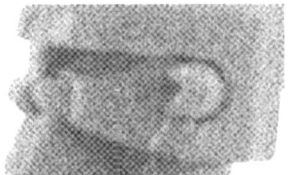

# DAY 4: FINDING SERENITY IN GOD'S PLAN

> *I have told you these things, so that in me you may have peace. In this world you will have trouble. But take heart! I have overcome the world.*
> *— John 16:33*

## REFLECTION

When I first became a Christian, I had the common misconception that when you follow Jesus, you are somehow protected from challenges and adversities. I quickly learned otherwise. Jesus Himself said, "In this world you will have trouble. But take heart! I have overcome the world" (John 16:33). Living for and like Jesus in our world today is one of the most challenging but rewarding things you can do. It is more dangerous than extreme sports and thrill rides; it is a full-contact sport. Jesus does not magically shield us from the storms of life, but He does give us the peace needed to sustain us through those storms that rage against and even within our very being.

As a young seminary student interning at an inner-city church, I married a woman who was also in seminary at the time and working in ministry. After a little over a year, the marriage was over. It was one of the most devastating storms in my life. The marriage ended in divorce due to my wife's infidelity. It rocked my world. I wanted to give up. I was in such a broken state that I didn't know if God could use me in ministry. But, through the love of God, church, small groups, and counseling, I found the serenity only Jesus can give. Peace is not only possible; it is ours to enjoy if we believe in God's word.

The "Serenity Prayer," often attributed to Reinhold Niebuhr, serves as a reminder of the significance of faith and acceptance when confronted with life's tribulations:

> God, grant me the serenity to accept the things I cannot change,
> Courage to change the things I can,
> And wisdom to know the difference.

Originating in the 1930s, it gained recognition and traction through various associations like Alcoholics Anonymous and other 12-step programs. Its straightforward yet profound message has made it central within diverse spiritual traditions, resonating with individuals from various backgrounds. The prayer captures the essence of the journey, seeking peace through faith, courage, and wisdom in keeping with God's divine plan.

The "Serenity Prayer" is an impactful expression that serves not only as a heartfelt request but also as a profound declaration of faith and a guide for leading a life centered on Christ. It begins by seeking peace and the ability to accept circumstances beyond our control, acknowledging our limitations and emphasizing the importance of trusting in God's sovereignty. It asks for the courage to make changes within our sphere of influence, encouraging us to act guided by God's wisdom. Lastly, it longs for wisdom to discern between these two realms, which is essential when faced with life's complexities.

This prayer is comprehensive. It encompasses the belief in a loving God who provides humility in times of strength, solace in moments of weakness, and clarity amidst chaos and confusion. When we recite these words, we are reminded to surrender our struggles to God's care, bravely embrace our calling and seek His guidance in every decision we make. "For with God nothing will be impossible" (Luke 1:37 NKJV).

# DOING THE INNER WORK

What aspects of your life do you feel cannot be changed?

Where do you feel called to make a change and need courage to take the next step?

Where do you need God's wisdom in discerning what is changeable and what is not?

# PRAYER FOCUS

---

Father in Heaven may the beautiful words of the "Serenity Prayer" touch my heart as I say them:

God, grant me the serenity to accept the things I cannot change,

Courage to change the things I can,

And wisdom to know the difference.

Lord, may I never lose sight of Your presence in my life. Guide me through every difficulty. Grant me the faith to surrender to Your plan. May Your steadfast love empower me. May I make decisions guided by the wisdom from You. I offer this prayer in the name of Jesus. Amen.

> *Nothing worth doing is completed in our lifetime; therefore, we must be saved by hope. Nothing true or beautiful or good makes complete sense in any immediate context of history; therefore, we must be saved by faith. Nothing we do, however virtuous, can be accomplished alone; therefore, we are saved by love.*
> *– Reinhold Niebuhr*

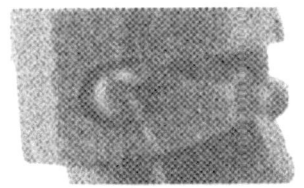

# DAY 5: EMBRACING STEP ONE - ADMITTING POWERLESSNESS

> *But he said to me, "My grace is sufficient for you, for my power is made perfect in weakness."*
> *– 2 Corinthians 12:9*

## STEP ONE: ADMIT POWERLESSNESS

## REFLECTION

We are a culture obsessed with power. Those who do not have power strive for it. Those who taste a bit of power want more and become insatiable. And those with a lot of power do not hesitate to weaponize it against those they lead. In the 18th century, Lord Acton, reflecting on the moral decay regarding the history of the Inquisition, wrote a series of letters to Bishop Creighton, an Archbishop of the Church of England, where his famous words ring true, *"Power tends to corrupt and absolute power corrupts absolutely."*[1]

---

1. Lord Acton, "Letter to Bishop Mandell Creighton," originally published April 5, 1887, Hanover College History Department, Hanover College, accessed November 18, 2023, https://history.hanover.edu/courses/excerpts/165acton.html.

Power reflects the growing narcissism of our times—marked by an insulated and individualistic drive to satisfy our own whims and desires without giving thought to the responsibility that goes with it. Power unchecked quickly leads to pride—perhaps one of the first significant sins. As Americans, we pride ourselves on rugged individualism by "picking ourselves up by our bootstraps." But our quest for power and individualism only leads to defeat. As Christ-followers, we acknowledge that as humans, we are powerless to overcome the sin in our own lives. The only way to find our freedom and true inner strength is by becoming weak and admitting to ourselves that we are truly powerless. When you reflect on your life, ask yourself, who or what has power over you? Is it your calendar, checkbook, finances, mind-altering substances, significant relationships, or just chasing the American dream? True fulfillment and victory come from admitting we are truly powerless.

Step One holds value not only for addressing alcoholism specifically but also for the various challenges that life presents. No soul is exempt from the pressures of life. Oftentimes, we find ourselves overwhelmed by compulsions, harmful behaviors, emotional wounds, and persistent hang-ups, despite our best efforts and intentions. It is important to note that this does not mean we are doomed to failure but rather that these behaviors are baked into our subconscious patterns.

But there is a way to break free of them, and it begins with Step One: recognizing our own powerlessness and human error. This does not signify weakness but the need for intervention and support. This initial step urges us to extend our gaze beyond our capabilities and rely on the strength and wisdom of a Supreme power to triumph over these difficulties. If it were possible for each man to be an island of self-sufficiency, nobody would be struggling against themselves. As earthly creatures, we can only do so much for ourselves before divine intervention becomes necessary. God designed us this way, so that all of our struggles point to a path that leads us back to Him.

Step One of Alcoholics Anonymous (AA) can serve as a starting point for anyone grappling with alcohol addiction or other deep-rooted issues. The first step involves acknowledging the lack of control we have over our situation and accepting that life has become unmanageable due to this struggle. It humbly beckons us to acknowledge our limitations while understanding that some aspects of life are beyond our influence. Therefore, these compel us to surrender to a Higher Power, namely God, in overcoming them. This is sometimes referred to as "radical acceptance." This sense of full acknowledgment and acceptance is at the very core of the 12 Steps.

# DOING THE INNER WORK

In what areas of your life do you feel powerless?

In what ways have you tried to change but have been unable to make those changes on your own?

It's scary to admit we are powerless. What makes this hard for you in your life? What are you afraid might happen if you admitted you were powerless?

## PRAYER FOCUS

Dear Lord, I openly admit that on my own I often struggle to bring about change. I humbly ask for Your grace to fill my gaps and for the humility to recognize my dependence on Your guidance and strength. Help me understand that when I feel most vulnerable, that's when Your power shows up. Grant me the courage to embark on this step toward healing and transformation, placing my trust in Your love and wisdom. In Jesus' name, Amen.

> *I do not understand the mystery of grace—only that it meets us where we are and does not leave us where it found us. – Anne Lamott*

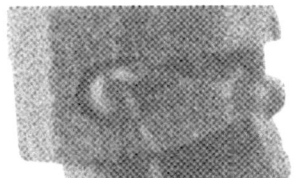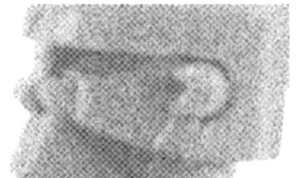

# DAY 6: TRUSTING IN JESUS

*One thing God has spoken, two things I have heard:*
*"Power belongs to you, God."*
*– Psalm 62:11*

## REFLECTION

The longer you live, the quicker you realize that people will fail you and let you down. Not just people but anything that humans touch—organizations, businesses, systems, politics, and even the church. Trust is difficult to gain or give. It takes many bricks to build its foundation, yet it can crumble in an instant. When we have experienced disappointments, our hearts can become so hardened that it can become difficult to want to trust anyone.

When we look at the life of Jesus, who was fully human and fully God, we also see one who was rejected by His own. He did not meet the expectations of His people for a political messiah, and He infuriated the religious elite of His culture. And yet, Jesus' words always matched His actions. The example we can follow is that He would often retreat to be alone with the one He trusted completely, His Heavenly Father. It may be challenging to want to change anything or anybody because of our hurt, pain, and trauma, but Jesus extends to all of us the invitation to put our whole trust in Him. We can take Jesus at His word and trust His promise never to leave or forsake us. Do you have difficulty trusting? It's time to admit that to God and develop a trusting relationship.

Understanding and acknowledging our lack of control allows us to embrace and nurture faith in God. This step recognizes that forces are at work beyond our volition and influence. It's a surrender to the reality that we don't have all the solutions and require assistance beyond our capabilities. Trusting in Jesus as our source of power supports and directs us toward a life of serenity guided by His love and wisdom.

The first step of the 12 Steps therefore encourages us to acknowledge the truth of our powerlessness when faced with the challenges that make our lives unmanageable. It's not about giving up. No, it's a humbling acceptance of our limitations and the recognition that we need to rely on a higher power. Within Christianity, this higher power is embodied by Jesus Christ. By admitting our inability to fend for ourselves independently, we become receptive to the strength and guidance offered by Jesus.

# DOING THE INNER WORK

What makes trust hard for you? In what circumstances have you trusted before and been let down?

What might happen if you tried trusting God with your life?

## PRAYER FOCUS

Lord Jesus, I humbly acknowledge my limitations and the need for Your strength in my life. Grant me the ability to realize my powerlessness when faced with challenges and to place my trust in You. As I take this course of surrender, please guide me with Your wisdom. Envelop me with Your comforting peace. Show me how to depend on You in all areas of my life so that I may discover the serenity and guidance that I earnestly desire from within You. May it be so, Amen.

> *When a train goes through a tunnel and it gets dark, you don't throw away the ticket and jump off. You sit still and trust the engineer. – Corrie Ten Boom*

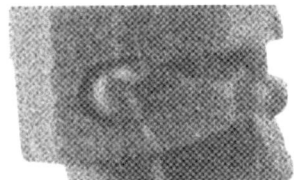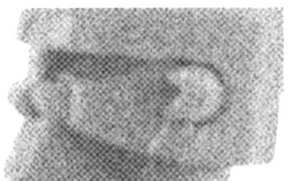

# DAY 7: SURRENDERING CONTROL FOR DIVINE GUIDANCE

> *In their hearts humans plan their course, but the LORD establishes their steps.*
> *– Proverbs 16:9*

## REFLECTION

I am not going to mince words here. You and I have control issues. We want to control our destiny and manage everything in and out of our power to bend everything to our will. It is our natural inclination to want to do so. That way, we won't have to leave our comfort zones, and we can focus solely on doing what we desire.

When I was experiencing a call to vocational ministry and was taking those next steps, I enlisted first in the United States Marine Corps Reserves and then the United States Navy. Here I was commissioned with the plan of going on active duty as a Chaplain. I had to go to seminary to do that, so that was the plan after getting my grades up and being accepted into seminary. But something happened along the way. I fell in love with the local church while doing an internship. I felt the pull to be a pastor, which transitioned into church planting and revitalization. Along the way, I had to give up what I thought the original plan was going to be for God's preferred future for my life. I believed I was going backward or settling because I did not want to deal with what I incorrectly deemed to be "mundane" church experiences at the time.

But God surprised me with an exciting adventure I would not even have conceived of then. Surrendering control over my own life was not easy. I was questioned, and I lamented giving up on what I thought was my dream. But God was guiding me as I sought direction. I did not know all the steps before me but decided to do the next right thing, which is what they teach you in recovery. *Where must you surrender control of your plans for God's divine guidance?* This is what we will delve into now.

Throughout our lives, we frequently strive to gain control and assurance to guide our course toward the results we strive for. However, this quest can make us dissatisfied and disillusioned when things do not play out the way we want them to. Personal development requires us to acknowledge that this desire for control is a human tendency aimed at dealing with life's twists and turns. True freedom is letting go of this craving for control and instead placing our trust in Jesus to guide our journey.

By surrendering our grip on this need for power, we realize that we cannot guarantee the results even though we formulate meticulous plans. Surrender is the act of release that allows us to balance action and being open-minded toward God's unfolding design.

This balance does not promote lethargy. Instead, it inspires us to trust in the God who desires to be in relationship with us and lead us through all of the valleys of life. This surrender alone can ease much of the unnecessary anxiety we carry about ourselves and the future, eliminating the need for emotional crutches and escapism.

# DOING THE INNER WORK

In what area(s) of your life do you need to surrender control?

What step(s) do you need to take to surrender your plans over to God?

# HEALING EXERCISE

Take some time to find a spot where you can reflect—the favorite part of your home, outdoors, or even church. Think about an aspect of your life that you've been trying to control. Once you've identified it, write it down on paper, acknowledging all the energy and effort you've put into trying to gain control over it. The simple act of putting pen to paper and writing out the issue will remove some of its weight.

Now take a breath. As you exhale, visualize yourself surrendering this situation to God. Picture yourself letting go of the paper, whether by placing it in a flowing river, burying it, or even safely burning it. While doing so, affirm to yourself: "I release my plans and trust in the guidance that will lead me forward."

Let this action symbolize your willingness to let go of control and have faith in God's guidance. As you move forward, know that your path is being guided for your benefit. Remember that, while our planning and efforts are typical aspects of life, the overall direction and unfolding are orchestrated by almighty God. So, continue making plans and working diligently toward your goals while remaining open-minded and adaptable to how God can shape your journey. It might be that reaching your goals leads to unforeseen challenges, or your plans result in unexpected and adverse outcomes. But God sees it all, and you must trust that He will reward your efforts in the best possible manner. Or it might be that a plan you had never considered suddenly comes into view, and it is the best thing for you. God is the ultimate planner.

# PRAYER FOCUS

Lord, I admit that I often try to take control of everything in my life. Today, I've decided to let go of an aspect of my life where I've been holding on tightly. I'm putting this situation in Your hands, trusting in Your guidance and wisdom.

Grant me peace as I release my grip, and instill in me the confidence to rely on Your plan and will for my life. I yield my aspirations for Your desires. So be it. In Jesus' Name, Amen.

> *God is God. Because He is God, He is worthy of my trust and obedience. I will find rest nowhere but in His holy will, that is unspeakably beyond my largest notions of what He is up to. – Elisabeth Elliot*

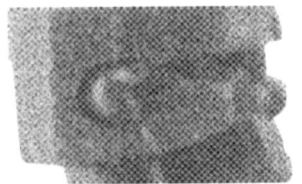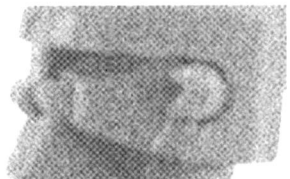

# DAY 8: EMBRACING TRUST IN STEP TWO

* * * * * * * * * * * * * * * * * * * * * * * * * * * * * * *

> *Come to me, all you who are weary and burdened, and I will give you rest. Take my yoke upon you and learn from me, for I am gentle and humble in heart, and you will find rest for your souls.*
> *— Matthew 11:28-29*

**STEP TWO: EMBRACE TRUST**

## REFLECTION

Einstein's purported definition of insanity is "doing the same thing over and over again and expecting different results." Whether or not he actually said this, there's some truth to it. Since humans are always in the pursuit of happiness, the true definition of insanity is "doing what we think will bring us happiness, fulfillment, and joy over and over again, only to realize these pursuits only serve as an escape from something we're trying to avoid or evade."

We can drive ourselves crazy chasing what the world tells us is the definition of success. That's why too much of a good thing can be detrimental. I have seen people striving for achievement, accolades, notoriety, and money, who get caught up in the rat race running on a "hamster wheel" of sorts. Tired as they are, they feel trapped and can't get off of it, even though no one is making them run—except themselves. It's a never-ending roller coaster that makes us sick, but we feel like we can't stop. The adrenaline-driven chase has caused us to become addicted to what we perceive to be an acceptable way of life. It means we can appear to be successful on the outside, but we are feeling like hell on the inside.

If that's you, know that Jesus came to restore us to sanity. The demands and expectations of ourselves and from others have left us operating out of a false sense of self. Our restoration can bring us freedom from all the inside and outside influences when we surrender to God's will for our lives.

As we enter this day of our guide, Step Two encourages us to embrace the idea of surrender from a Christian perspective. Surrendering in this context does not imply defeat—rather, it is centered on finding solace, serenity, and security by entrusting our lives to Jesus. He is the higher power capable of restoring harmony to our chaotic world.

Take a moment to contemplate what surrender means to you personally within your journey. Recall instances when letting go led to tranquility. Reflect on the burdens that weigh heavily on you and how they affect your life and relationship with God. Recognize that surrendering isn't a sign of giving up—rather, it's an act of faith where you give over all your concerns and struggles to Jesus. Examine any hesitancy or reluctance you might have toward embracing this surrender. Reflect on what it would take for you to let go of this hesitation and place your trust in Jesus' ability to guide and restore you.

Matthew 11:28-29 allows us an opportunity to reflect on the image of Jesus, not as a task master but as a compassionate Savior, eagerly willing to help bear the weight of our troubles. Meditating on His promise of rest can bring comfort and hope. Imagine how this commitment from Jesus to help you bear your burdens could become a reality to bring you healing and a renewed spirit. Just the idea of releasing your worries to Him can bring about change.

# DOING THE INNER WORK

What burdens are you carrying?

Name the ones you are ready to surrender to Jesus.

# PRAYER FOCUS

Dear Heavenly Father, I come before You today in the name of Jesus to embrace Step Two. I acknowledge my powerlessness. I recognize that I need Your divine intervention. I surrender all my burdens, struggles, and worries to You. Please guide me in letting go of my desire for control. Help me place my trust in Your power to restore and heal. Grant me the ability to find rest and peace in You during weariness and confusion. May You always remind me of Your promise to provide peace, strength, comfort, and unfailing love. May this surrender lead me toward a renewed and deeper faith in You. Amen.

> *Job one is get out of that cave. A lot of people do get out but don't change. – Robert Downey Jr.*

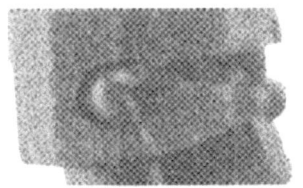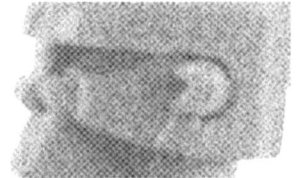

# DAY 9: CONVERSING WITH CHRIST IN PRAYER

> *Then you will call on me and come and pray to me, and I will listen to you.*
> *– Jeremiah 29:12*

## REFLECTION

The Christian life is more than believing in Jesus as the Higher Power. It means developing a personal relationship with Him. The ways we draw close to Jesus in our lives are known to Methodists in particular as the "means of grace." Prayer is a primary means of grace.

Often, we complicate prayer because we think it involves changing our communication style to become someone we are not. But prayer simply means communicating with God. In the Gospels, the disciples could have asked Jesus to teach them anything: how to get rich, be happy, start a movement, and influence people, but they asked Jesus to teach them how to pray. Sounds complicated, but Jesus gave us a straightforward and personal example in The Lord's Prayer.

Communication means expressing our feelings and emotions. More important than speaking, communication involves active listening. Jesus would often get away from the crowds to retreat and pray. He practiced this kind of intimacy with the Heavenly Father. When all we do is talk, it is impossible to listen. If we stay busy all the time and do not slow down, it becomes harder to resist the distractions that keep us from forming a relationship.

During the pandemic, we learned there was a silver lining for our family. We got to enjoy more mealtimes with our three girls. But in order for us to be more present, my wife, Callie, would gently remind me to get off my phone or not give in to a knee-jerk reaction when it lit up from a notification. During these small moments, I realized that I was prioritizing my own busyness over my relationships. Take time today to get away from the noise of life, even if it is a quiet place in your house. Put away all your technology, turn off the TV, and talk to and listen to Jesus.

On this day of our journey, as we explore Step Two more deeply, we shift our attention to prayer. Instead of perceiving it as a ceremony, we approach prayer as an open and sincere conversation with our Higher Power, Jesus Christ. Picture this prayer as a dialogue where you can freely share your experiences, hopes, and fears and express your gratitude.

Imagine engaging in a conversation with Jesus. What would you discuss if you could speak candidly and openly over tea, for example? Take pleasure in sharing both the joys and struggles of your life, expressing your aspirations and intimate concerns just like you would with a close companion.

Jeremiah 29:12 underscores the significance of communication and how valuable our voice and ears are in our relationship with God. As you ponder upon this verse, remember that your prayers are not words spoken into the void, but they are heard and cherished by our Lord Jesus.

# DOING THE INNER WORK

Where can you find a quiet place and time in which you can talk with Jesus?

What helps you quiet your mind and listen?

What distractions do you intentionally have to avoid?

Take some time right now to talk with God. Share honestly and listen. If you've never heard God speak before, notice if a word, phrase, image, or scripture verse comes to mind in the stillness. Hold it lightly. Does this sound like the voice of your Heavenly Father who loves you? Does it line up with what you've read in the Bible? Scripture can be a guide as you start to recognize God's voice. Don't get discouraged if it takes time to start to recognize His voice. The more you talk with God and listen for Him, the more familiar His voice becomes.

# PRAYER FOCUS

Dear Jesus, I want to express my appreciation to You for being a source of comfort and guidance in my life. Today, I come before You with sincerity and an open heart to share the highs and lows of my day. I am truly grateful for everything You've done for me. I humbly ask for Your blessing, seek Your assistance in dealing with the range of emotions I experience, and look to You to guide me as I make decisions. With unwavering trust, I place my hopes, dreams, and fears in Your hands, knowing that You will always light up the path ahead. Amen.

> *I pray that you all put your shoes way under the bed at night so that you gotta get on your knees in the morning to find them. And while you're down there, thank God for grace and mercy and understanding.*
> *– Denzel Washington*

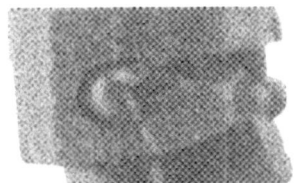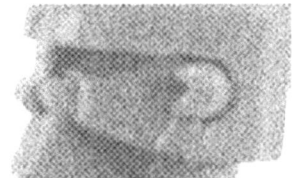

# DAY 10: FINDING PEACE IN TRUST

I sought the LORD, and he answered me;
he delivered me from all my fears.
– Psalm 34:4

## REFLECTION

Whenever you turn on the TV, read a news article, or hop on social media, the underlying message says: "Be afraid; be very afraid." It is possible to become so paralyzed with fear that somehow, in our "stinkin' thinkin," we start to believe everything is out of control. And yet, Jesus, our ultimate Higher Power, wants to give us the power to experience freedom in a world bound by fear.

Fear and worry go hand in hand. They breed and feed on each other. But note that what we fear and worry about is in the past or future. It has already happened to us or someone we know, or it is something which will likely never happen. Yet we get obsessed about it when we go down the "what if" path.

On the other hand, when we place our trust in Jesus Christ, we can find peace. The Hebrew word for peace is *sha-*

*lom,* which expands a narrow definition of "tranquility" to a more holistic meaning. *Shalom* is used 250 times in the Hebrew Bible, which Old Testament scholar, Hugh Whelchel, breaks down into three catagories: it is used 10 percent of the time as a farewell or greeting, 25 percent of the time in the context of relational conflicts or tensions, but 65 percent of the time "shalom refers to completeness, maturity, and especially overall well-being economically, relationally, and physically."[1] It takes on new meaning when we apply the title of Prince of Peace to Jesus because we declare our trust for all areas of our lives in His perfect *shalom.*

With this context in mind, as we near the completion of Step Two in the 12 Steps, we look into strengthening our faith in Jesus, our Higher Power. This step emphasizes the belief that Jesus can bring stability and peace into the areas of our lives where fear and uncertainty have dominated.

Take a moment to contemplate how embracing Jesus as your Higher Power has impacted your experience of fear and anxiety. Reflect on instances from the past when your fears were alleviated or transformed through your trust in Him. Additionally, consider the broader significance of clarity, purpose, and inner peace within Step Two. Recall moments when relying on Jesus brought serenity into situations.

Psalm 34:4 serves as a reminder that it's not just about being heard but also about divine intervention. We can draw connections to Step Two with Psalm 34:4. Reaching out to Jesus can result in freedom from the tumultuous grip of fear. It's a realization that we're never alone and there is always hope and freedom awaiting us when we seek solace in Him.

---

1.     Hugh Whelchel, "What Is Shalom According to the Bible?" *Institute for Faith, Work, and Economics,* accessed November 19, 2023, https://tifwe.org/what-is-shalom-according-to-the-bible/.

# DOING THE INNER WORK

Take a moment to focus on what you know to be true about God… His goodness, grace, love, mercy, kindness, and peace. Where have you seen God's goodness in your life?

When you focus on God and God's goodness in your life, how does it change your level of anxiety? When you move from a focus on your problems to a focus on the One who can solve them, peace should increase, and fear should decrease.

Worship music can help shift our focus from our problems to God. Take a few minutes to listen to worship music. What is your peace level after listening to some worship music? Is there a song that you need to listen to regularly in this season?

# HEALING EXERCISE

Recognizing and releasing our fears to God can impact our lives. Whether it's a momentary concern or a more profound anxiety, taking the time to acknowledge and let go of it can bring us a sense of peace and clarity. So why not take a moment today to identify and surrender your fears to Jesus? Write them down on a piece of paper, your journal, or right here in the margins of the page.

*Prayer Focus*

Jesus, as I contemplate Step Two, I have faith in Your ability to bring peace, clarity, and understanding into my life. I acknowledge how my trust in You can allay my anxieties. Help me in releasing my fears to You so that I may experience the comfort of Your presence and guidance. Grant me the courage to place my fears at Your feet. In Jesus' name, Amen.

> *I have come to believe that my true identity is not found in the expression of my will but in the submission to God's. – Russell Brand.*

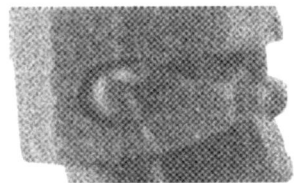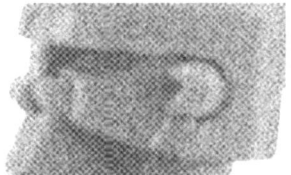

# DAY 11: EMBRACING SURRENDER IN STEP THREE

* * * * * * * * * * * * * * * * * * * * * * * * * * * * * * * * * * *

> *Teach me to do your will, for you are my God; may your good Spirit lead me on level ground.*
> **– Psalm 143:10**

**STEP THREE: FIND STRENGTH IN SURRENDER**

## REFLECTION

Committing to follow Jesus may start by giving God an hour of our worship on a Sunday. This hopefully blossoms into a deeper intimacy with God as we invest daily time in nurturing this relationship. The Christian life is about making Jesus not only the Savior who can and will save us from our sins but also the Lord of our lives. Lordship means we offer God our whole selves—our time, talent, and treasure. It is turning our will over to God. It is no longer operating in the way the world has tried to program into us; instead, it is operating according to God's will and Word.

To know God's will is to cultivate a relationship with Him.

Giving Jesus lordship over our lives means surrendering our former and entire life, knowing that God's best is better than our best thinking and desires. It starts with an initial decision to claim Jesus as Savior and Lord, but it also involves making conscious decisions daily. It means we bring everything to God in life's decision processes. God is not a distant, far-off God in the universe but a personal God who desires to have an intimate relationship with you.

This idea of surrender is genuinely intriguing, especially regarding our life's journey. It can seem counterintuitive or even unsettling at times. However, it can bring us freedom. Surrendering doesn't imply weakness. Rather it acknowledges our limitations. Sometimes, the most merciful action we can take for ourselves is surrendering. It shows a willingness to seek guidance from the One who has all wisdom and knowledge and power.

When we think about handing over our will to God, mixed emotions are bound to arise. On the one hand, we have the fear of relinquishing control and relying on someone other than ourselves. On the other hand, a sense of peace settles upon us in the knowledge that God has a plan, and we don't have to manage everything alone. It serves as a reminder to have faith and trust in a path that surpasses our understanding of life when instinctively we want to hold onto control and are hesitant about losing our independence.

In Psalm 143:10 we find a prayer for guidance and movement toward the future—a path illuminated by the Holy Spirit's wisdom. As you reflect upon this scripture, consider those areas where God's guidance could assist you in overcoming challenges and guiding you toward a journey of self-actualization and recovery.

# DOING THE INNER WORK

What feelings and emotions arise in you when you think about surrendering control to God?

Have you made the decision to have God not just as Savior but as Lord of your life? If so, what did that change look like? Feel like? If not, I invite you to consider that step of surrender now, as you offer your whole life to God.

Are there any areas of your life that you are still trying to control that you haven't surrendered to God? What would it look like and feel like to surrender those areas to the Lord?

# PRAYER FOCUS

Lord, today I come to You with a reflection of Step Three, seeking Your wisdom to understand the meaning of surrender. From the depths of my heart, I ask for Your help so that I can let go of my plans and confidently embrace the future You've crafted for me. Give me the strength to surrender my will to You each day and grant me the courage to place my trust in Your loving care, knowing that Your plans are greater than mine. Thank You for listening to my prayer. Amen.

> *The most important thing I've learned in sobriety is that I have absolutely no control over other people's behavior. I only have control over my reaction to it.*
> *— Kristen Johnston*

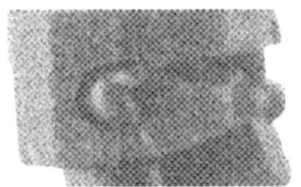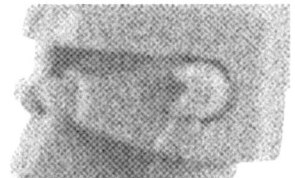

# DAY 12: FINDING STRENGTH IN SURRENDER

*Father, if you are willing, take this cup from me; yet not my will, but yours be done.*
*– Luke 22:42*

## REFLECTION

Today's scripture shares one of Jesus' loneliest moments in the Garden of Gethsemane. In His hour of dire distress, He asked the disciples to stay up with Him that night and pray, but they fell asleep and weren't there for Him. Jesus knew what the Father was asking Him to do. In fact, He had been preparing His entire life for the fate He was going to encounter on the Cross. But now He was in such agony that blood instead of sweat came out of His pores. The moment's intensity brought a painful dialogue Jesus was having in prayer. But His final answer to the Father was this: "Not My will, but Yours be done." With that exchange, it was a done deal.

Finalized, Jesus surrendered His will to God. It was yet another moment in which He found strength in surrender.

When was the last time you submitted your will to God, especially when it came to a complex and even painful decision? Examine your life. In what areas do you need to surrender and find real strength?

As we move further into Step Three, the concept of willingness becomes prominent. Willingness is pivotal in surrendering to God Almighty and entrusting our lives to Him. This signifies a subtle yet impactful shift from *control* to *trust*. It entails transitioning from relying on our will to embracing God's guidance. It is important to assess our readiness to surrender our will to God. Are there any reservations we have that hold us back, such as fears, doubts, or concerns about losing our sense of self? Remember that willingness doesn't mean being fearless but being willing to move on despite our fears. Some might call this "courage."

Take some time today for introspection. Identify what you might be clinging to. What is causing you to hesitate? Acknowledge these obstacles. Contemplate the freedom that could be yours by letting go of them.

Luke 22:42 describes the struggle Jesus faced when confronted with the suffering He would endure. It's a normal reaction to try to avoid pain. But at base, Jesus understood that it was all part of God's plan. As we reflect on this scripture, we recognize moments when we've had to surrender our desires and embrace what God had in store for us. It's not always easy, but we understand the significance of placing our trust in God's plan.

# DOING THE INNER WORK

Sit with some of the questions from the reflection. When was the last time you submitted your will to God, especially when it came to a complex and even painful decision?

In what areas do you need to surrender and find real strength?

Are there any reservations holding you back such as fears and doubts or concerns about losing your sense of self? What might you be clinging onto?

What examples can we find in the Word that strengthen our trust in God's faithfulness?

# PRAYER FOCUS

Dear God, as I proceed with Step Three, I ask for Your help in surrendering my will to Yours. Grant me the courage to release control and have faith in Your guidance. May I discover resilience in my vulnerability and confidently declare, "Not my will, but Yours be done" too. In Jesus' name I offer this prayer. Amen.

> *Carry the cross patiently, and with perfect submission; and in the end it shall carry you.*
> *– Thomas à Kempis*

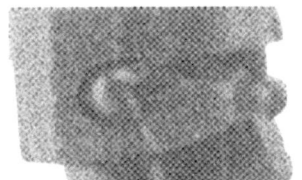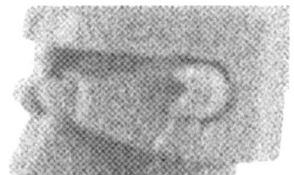

# DAY 13: TRUSTING GOD WITH CONTROL

> *Commit to the* LORD *whatever you do,*
> *and he will establish your plans.*
> *— Proverbs 16:3*

## REFLECTION

When we are in a trusted, committed relationship, we show our love by being intentional in our words and actions. That could mean breaking away from the past and the culture of our family of origin. It could also mean seeking healing from the trauma that could derail our present and future.

When I became a husband and then a father, I knew I wanted to be different than what was modeled in my family of origin. Sometimes, life's greatest lessons are learning what *not* to do and how *not* to act. My primary role is being a child of God. It takes intentionality to be in a relationship with God our Heavenly Father. My other roles are also important. I cannot be the father and husband I want to be if I am not intentionally seeking to commit my ways to God. It is through God that we become less selfish. We learn that, although we have our rights, so do our loved ones—and we need to honor them too. You and I need daily wisdom from God to be who we intend to be and not who the world wants us to be. Intentionality means putting our whole trust in God and seeking His ways that are better than our own.

As we journey further into the third step, we are confronted with the necessity of relinquishing authority to Jesus Christ, our Supreme Power. This stage implores us to put on faith and to acknowledge that we are not in command of our own fate.

Dedicate some time today to reflect on elements of your life in which you grapple with surrendering control. Think about your aspirations, relationships, challenges, or achievements. Look within yourself to understand why releasing control in these areas is difficult. Is it because of fear of the unknown or a belief that only you can ensure a particular outcome? Consider the possibility that Jesus has greater capability than we can fathom to deal with these issues empathetically and wisely.

Proverbs 16:3 reminds us that entrusting our actions to Jesus doesn't mean giving up on our hopes or responsibilities. Instead, it invites Jesus to be a partner in our endeavors. As we meditate on this verse, let's take a moment to reflect on what it genuinely means to commit our actions by letting God shape our plans.

# DOING THE INNER WORK

What does trust look like to you in a committed friendship and relationship?

How might trust be difficult for you based on past experiences?

# HEALING EXERCISE

It is crucial to make time for introspection and meditation. Try visualizing yourself clutching onto facets of your life and then imagine gradually yielding them up to Jesus. You may actually want to clench your hands physically and then slowly release them with the open palms of your hands facing up in a posture of openness and surrender. Be aware of the emotions surfacing during this exercise. Do you feel trepidation? Or relief and peace? Conclude with a moment of silence while acknowledging that support from Jesus is always available. He will guide and uphold you through each step toward releasing control.

This practice hinges on understanding that surrendering power does not render us helpless but aligns us more closely to God's will for our lives.

## PRAYER FOCUS

Dear Lord, as I contemplate trusting You wholly with my life, help me experience freedom from the areas where letting go proves difficult. Teach me to rely on Your wisdom, knowing well that submission before You isn't a sign of weakness but resonates with Your character and nature. In the name of Jesus, Amen.

> *Surrendering to God is not passive resignation, fatalism, or an excuse for laziness. It may mean the exact opposite: sacrificing your life or suffering in order to change what needs to be changed. – Rick Warren*

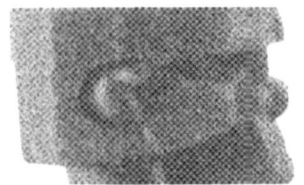

# DAY 14: EMBRACING SELF-REFLECTION IN STEP FOUR

> *The LORD is my light and my salvation—*
> *whom shall I fear? The LORD is the stronghold of my life—*
> *of whom shall I be afraid?*
> *– Psalm 27:1*

**STEP FOUR: EMBRACE SELF-REFLECTION**

## REFLECTION

It is easy to wear our busyness as a badge of honor in our society and the church. We're a culture that values "hard work," and being busy gives us the sense of being productive. But underneath, the need to stay active and not sit still in inertia is more profound. As a self-identified achiever who is always moving on from project to project, checking the boxes on a to-do list in a hurry, I know that the shadow side of my personality is workaholism. I also recognize it's because I am running from something. What I am running from is not a situation or person. I am often running from what's inside.

When we have unresolved trauma, we internalize it, and it manifests in different ways. Some run to the numbing effects of drugs, alcohol, binge-watching media, shopping, over-eating, or other forms of addiction. Others try to busy themselves with work, helping others, or pressuring their kids to live differently, so their children never experience what they lived through.

When we reflect and meditate on our past and even our present-day realities, we may be surprised by how we feel. When we take time for reflection, meditation, and devotion, we could be surprised by what God reveals and speaks to us. Areas we need to work on require healing, as they manifest in the wrongs we have done and the wrongs we continue to do. Our actions tell us that a change is needed for our lives.

The fourth step therefore invites us on an introspective journey—prompting us to face those truths about ourselves that we often sidestep. It offers a chance for us to delve deeper into our character and investigate zones typically shrouded from our consciousness. This step requires courage, as our introspection could unveil profound fears, insecurities, and uncertainties.

The practice of self-awareness is not about reprimanding ourselves but rather gaining a more transparent comprehension of our identity. It's about coming clean, so that our shadow self does not surface when we operate in unhealthy ways. As we prepare for this inward exploration, let us recognize any discomfort that may arise. Even though it's hard, this phase offers a chance for change and growth, revealing to us our own ability to adapt to life's changing circumstances and demands. It's about revealing our insecurities while uncovering our strengths, resilience, and capacity for change.

# DOING THE INNER WORK

What are you afraid of as you prepare to look under the surface of your life?

What image of yourself are you trying to protect that might come into question if you acknowledge your shortcomings?

# PRAYER FOCUS

Heavenly Father, guide me through Stage Four with Your wisdom. Give me the strength to confront my true self honestly. Help me to sift through my fears and uncertainties as I embark on this introspective moral inventory journey fearlessly yet cautiously. May Your wisdom guide me as I reflect upon my life experiences. May Psalm 27 be my source of comfort during times of doubt or fear. Help me learn from what I uncover about myself so that my healing can lead to transformation, enabling me to serve Your divine purpose better. In Jesus' name, I pray, Amen.

> *The most beautiful people we have known are those who have known defeat, known suffering, known struggle, known loss, and have found their way out of the depths. – Elisabeth Kübler-Ross*

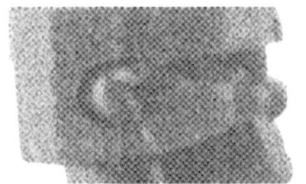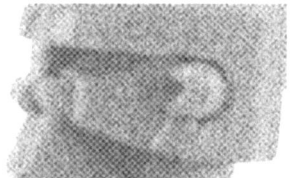

# DAY 15: COMMITTING TO SELF-DISCOVERY

## REFLECTION

Here's an important question—and it affects everything in your life. Have you ever taken the time to work on yourself? Not other people, places, or things, but just yourself, your challenges, and areas in which you want to grow? Committing to a journey of self-discovery is the greatest gift you can give yourself and those around you. Ask yourself, "What is it like being on the other side of me?" It's a simple question worth grappling with internally but also worth sharing with others.

The journey toward self-discovery paves the way for self-awareness. Engaging in this process can be beneficial when done alongside a spiritual mentor, sponsor, counselor, or even through journaling. This journey is not easy or for the faint of heart. It is much like beginning a physical fitness routine. When you start, you may not look forward to doing it. It costs you time (but it's actually an investment), and you will be sore with aches and pains. But when you develop consistency, you will begin to reap the rewards. You will feel revitalized with a new energy for your life and dreams. It is the gift that keeps on giving. The same is true when we commit to a life-long path of self-discovery.

As we progress with Step Four, it's important to bear in mind that this is a journey of self-exploration. It's not merely a one-time task or something that can be accomplished over-night. Embracing this journey entails being ready to confront any truths about ourselves that we might uncover, even if they're uncomfortable or challenging on a long-term basis. What are some of the things we can remind ourselves of or let go of in order to fully commit to this journey? Let's bear all these considerations in mind as we continue moving forward in our journey.

# DOING THE INNER WORK

What is it like being on the other side of myself?

What do I know to be true about God and God's love for me that can sustain me as I bravely go through this journey of self-discovery?

# PRAYER FOCUS

Dear Lord, as I continue on this journey, I commit myself to exploring and understanding my inner self. Please give me the courage and resilience to face the good, bad, and ugly within. Help me find Your love and mercy along this path, guiding me toward a life of healing and wholeness. In the name of Jesus, I pray, Amen.

> *The new codependency helps you understand that letting go of what you can't control is a major step towards peace of mind and heart. Your life can be transformed by letting go, focusing on what you can control, what you have, and what you want.*
> *– Melody Beattie*

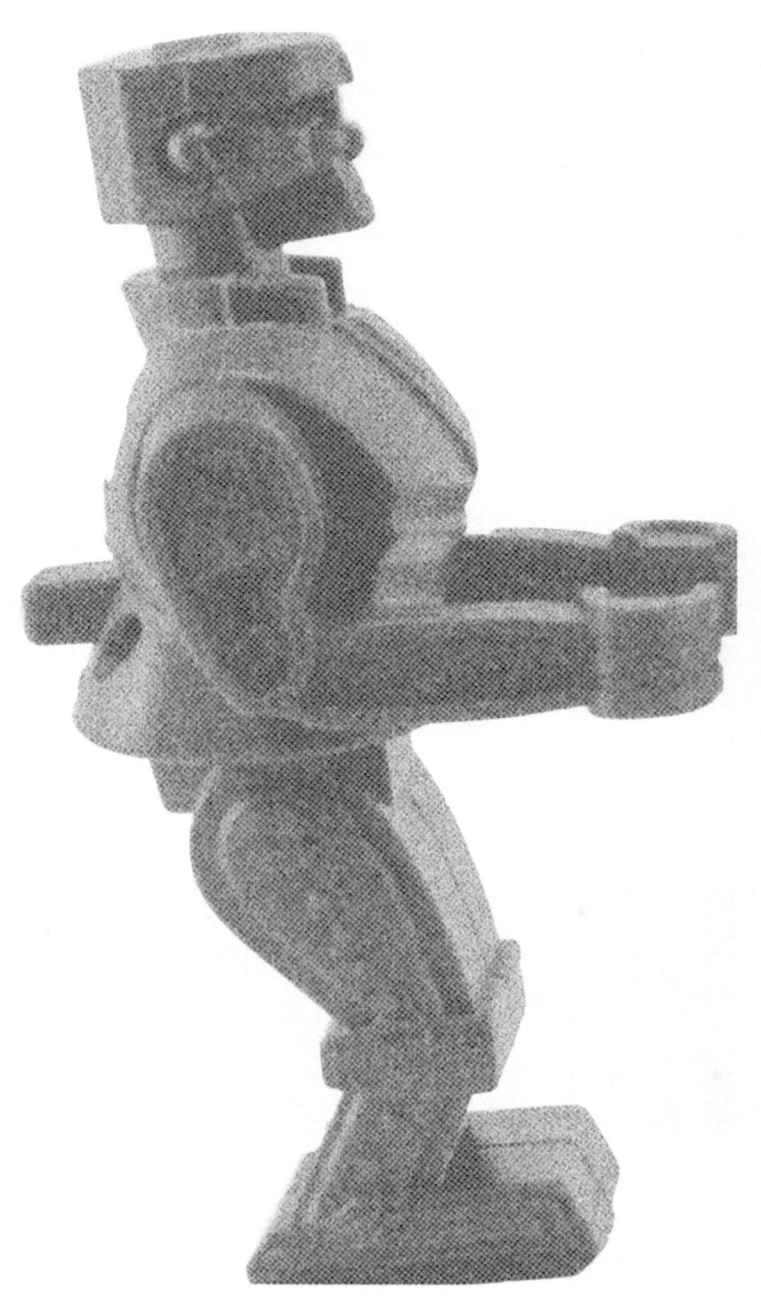

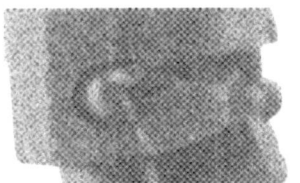

# DAY 16: ACKNOWLEDGING OUR MISSTEPS

> *But who can discern their own errors?*
> *Forgive my hidden faults.*
> *– Psalm 19:12*

## REFLECTION

Earlier, we saw how the word "sin," or *hamartia* in the New Testament Greek, can be defined as literally "missing the mark." Consider archery—a practice involving a bow and arrow aimed at a target with a red bullseye. Unless you're highly skilled, you might miss the mark to varying degrees. Even if you're just a centimeter away from the red dot, the reality remains: you've still missed it.

Sin is missing the mark with our worst–or even our best–intentions. The key to dealing with our missteps is acknowledging them before God and others. Usually, we have that inward conscience, or more properly, the Holy Spirit, which God uses to speak to our hearts when we have sinned badly or missed the mark. Usually, I know when I have hugely misstepped, but I need my quiet, alone time with God to see where I missed the mark in subtle ways.

Recognizing and taking responsibility for our mistakes, especially if they contradict our values or have caused harm to others, is of grave importance if we want a chance to change. In our journey of growth, we must honestly assess our imperfections and learn from our missteps. Instead of condemning ourselves, let's concentrate on gaining insights and readying ourselves to make amends. Take a moment to ponder situations where your actions may have fallen short of your ideals and contemplate their impact on both you and others. Then, take steps toward healing and righting any wrongs (more on this in the Days to come).

Psalm 19:12 reminds us that, as fallible beings, we often fail to acknowledge our faults and therefore require God's guidance to recognize them and seek His forgiveness. The psalm encourages us to seek God's assistance in understanding our mistakes and in giving us the grace and humility necessary to confront these truths and commit to positive change.

# DOING THE INNER WORK

Why is it difficult for us as human beings to acknowledge when we have missed the mark?

How can we go one step beyond acknowledging our missteps in moving toward forgiveness and healing?

# HEALING EXERCISE

To progress in this journey, begin by taking a pause. Sit still with yourself for a couple of minutes. Breathe slowly, in and out. Contemplate your actions while acknowledging any errors you might have made. Acknowledging the importance of growth and showing a genuine intent to rectify unwholesome situations is necessary. By documenting these acknowledgments, you demonstrate a willingness to seek forgiveness and healing and take measures toward reconciliation and self-improvement in your relationships with others.

# PRAYER FOCUS

God, as I move forward with Step Four, I humbly come before You to seek Your guidance in acknowledging and accepting my mistakes and weaknesses. I seek to fully understand their impact on others and our relationship. Grant me the strength to face these truths, and the wisdom to learn from them. Expressing my admissions in writing reveals my desire for growth and a genuine commitment to making amends. Your grace and forgiveness are instrumental on this journey of self-discovery and healing. Please lead me toward restoration so that I can embody Your love and compassion fully. In Jesus' name, I pray, Amen.

> *There is no greater agony than bearing an untold story inside you. – Maya Angelou*

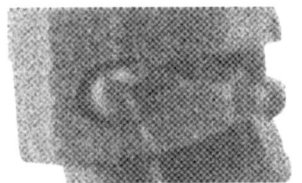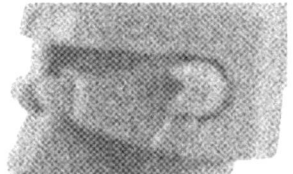

# DAY 17: EMBRACING HONESTY IN STEP FIVE

> *Therefore confess your sins to each other and pray for each other so that you may be healed.*
> *— James 5:16*

**STEP FIVE: ADMIT OUR WRONGDOINGS**

## REFLECTION

Honesty is a hard thing to come by. In my brief time as a parent of three little girls, I've found that if children do something they're not allowed to—like sneaking extra dessert or candy—they might resort to lying unless caught in the act. I'm less upset about their actions and more concerned about the act of lying itself. Often it is easier to be brutally honest with others than it is to be honest with ourselves. The hardest person to be truthful with is the reflection we see in the mirror. We have heard it said before, "We are only as sick as our secrets." But our dishonesty and hiding do not deceive God. It is time to come out of hiding and embrace honesty. The truth will set us free and bring healing to our lives.

Now, as we progress to Step Five, we must take the time to acknowledge the mistakes we've made, not just toward ourselves but also toward others and above all, toward God. Reflect on what it means to you personally to acknowledge your faults. Why is this admission vital as you continue on your path toward recovery and spiritual growth? Consider how embracing your imperfections can facilitate healing as you take personal responsibility and enhance connections with others and with God.

Reflecting on James 5:16, consider the role of confession in your life. Have you shared your struggles with someone trustworthy who can act as a sounding board for you? If not, consider how doing so could strengthen your faith and bring healing.

# DOING THE INNER WORK

Are you ready to be set free through confession? What are you afraid of?

Who are some safe people you could share your struggles with? Look for people who are mature and will love you and help you receive God's forgiveness.

# PRAYER FOCUS

God, as I move forward with Step Five, I humbly ask for Your guidance and strength. Give me the courage to recognize my mistakes and take responsibility for them. Help me understand the importance of this step in my journey toward healing and personal growth, knowing that this process will bring relief, deeper healing, and a stronger connection with You.

Grant me the wisdom to choose someone I trust with whom I can openly share my confession.

May Your presence empower me to confront the truth about my actions. May acknowledging my wrongdoing bring clarity, accountability, and a renewed sense of purpose in my life. I offer this prayer in Jesus' name. Amen.

> *Owning our story and loving ourselves through that process is the bravest thing we'll ever do.*
> *— Brené Brown*

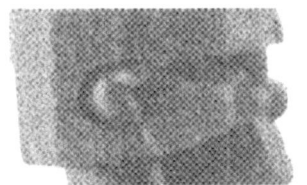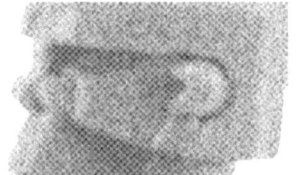

# DAY 18: THE LIBERATION
# OF ADMISSION

> *Whoever conceals their sins does not prosper, but the one*
> *who confesses and renounces them finds mercy.*
> *– Proverbs 28:13*

## REFLECTION

You do not have to be confined behind cell bars to be locked up. You can be in a prison of your mind. People are bound to all types of things; each one picks his or her prison. Substance abuse calls for the most attention. Yet, as you've probably discovered, anything can take mastery over us. We may mistakenly believe we can control and own "it," but it ultimately manages and owns us. When the addiction is to material items, we need to remember that our possessions can possess us.

One aspect of Jesus' earthly ministry—which continues today in His followers—is bringing freedom to the captives (Isaiah 61:1-4). We all need to be liberated from sin. Scripture is clear: confession is one of the primary ways to gain freedom. We can experience God's power in confession. I have witnessed that. When one person confesses his or her missteps, others begin opening up. I have seen this in small group settings and experienced it in friendships and at recovery services. Free people want to help others become free. Admission is hard and painful, and naturally, we don't want to admit our wrongs. But when we do, we shed the weight of something we have carried around with us that's rotting inside. For some, that weight has been an accumulation of years. No matter how long, God can and will give us freedom when we cry out to Him.

On Day 18, we acknowledge the significance of owning our mistakes. By admitting our faults, we can unburden ourselves of the lingering guilt and shame that sits beneath our conscience. With it, we can embrace genuine honesty and vulnerability. This act of admission not only brings a sense of relief and freedom, but it also aids in healing and restoring our relationships with others. Think about the weight lifting off your shoulders when you no longer hide your errors but instead embrace truth and responsibility. Reflect on the clarity that accompanies this process of admission.

Proverbs 28:13 is a verse that highlights the importance of being truthful about our mistakes and weaknesses. It reminds us that concealing our wrongdoings only leads to harmful consequences, while confessing them and renouncing them will bring us grace and forgiveness. It can also make us feel less alone in our struggles against sin. Take a moment to consider areas where you might be hiding your mistakes or shortcomings. Reflect on how you can gather the courage to confess these behaviors and distance yourself from them. Keep in mind that mercy and understanding are always available when we choose honesty and accountability.

## DOING THE INNER WORK

What areas of your life are you hiding? What sins bring you the most shame?

How would life be different if you didn't have to carry that shame any longer?

# PRAYER FOCUS

Dear God, guide me as I move through Step Five. Help me admit my wrongs to You and those I trust and give me the strength to face my mistakes with honesty and humility. Your word teaches that confession leads to Your mercy, so may this process deepen my self-awareness and draw me closer to You. Let Your love and mercy be my constant comfort and strength. In Jesus' name, Amen.

> *I don't have a drinking problem. I have a thinking problem. – Craig Ferguson*

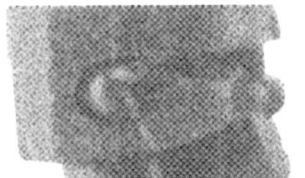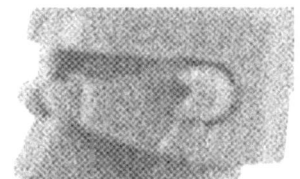

# DAY 19: FINDING TRUST AND SUPPORT

> *Carry each other's burdens, and in this way*
> *you will fulfill the law of Christ.*
> **– Galatians 6:2**

## REFLECTION

We cannot live this life alone—especially the Christian life. It's a team sport with Jesus as our captain. There are no superstars, MVPs, or individual stats because we are only as strong as how the team performs. John Wesley, the founder of the Methodist movement, put it this way succinctly: "There is no holiness but social holiness." Our salvation is more than just *me, myself, and I*, a theme that pervades popular culture. No, it's not me but *we*. Attempting to recover our lives is more than just turning our will over to God. It means allowing a community of faith to help shape us. And though we may not be able to choose our family of origin, we can select our community—and we must choose wisely.

I once heard this statistic from Jim Rohn, "You are the average of the five people you spend the most time with.[1]" If all we do is spend time with folks enveloped in negativity, drama, and bad attitudes, then it comes as no surprise that they will start to influence us, whether we are consciously aware of it or not. Finding trust and support can be difficult. It can be challenging, but I look for signs of the fruit of the Holy Spirit in their lives. Those fruit found in Galatians 5:22-23 are, "love, joy, peace, forbearance, kindness, goodness, faithfulness, gentleness and self-control." The people who display such fruit are the ones I aim to surround myself with and emulate.

Who makes up your inner circle? Are they lifting you up or dragging you down?

As we move forward together to Step Five, we consider in greater measure who we can choose to confide in. This decision carries weight as it requires trust, understanding, and discretion. Contemplate who in your life could fulfill this role. It might be a sponsor, a trusted friend, or even a spiritual mentor—anyone with whom you place a lot of trust. Consider the qualities that make someone a trustworthy confidante: empathy, discretion, and wisdom. Reflect on the comfort and trust you feel with this person and how that person's guidance and support can aid you on your path toward healing and personal growth.

Galatians 6:2 sheds light on the significance of support and care in our journey. Take a moment for introspection on how confiding in someone is in keeping with this principle of support.

---

1.     Jim Rohn, *The Art of Exceptional Living* (New York, NY: Nightingale-Conant, 1993), audio program.

# DOING THE INNER WORK

What qualities and characteristics do you look for in the supporting cast who makes up your inner circle?

Who are the people that should be in your supporting cast?

# HEALING EXERCISE

Take a moment to think about the individuals in your life who could provide support to you. Take note of the names of those you believe would be suitable for engaging in a conversation about your personal victories and struggles. Consider their qualities, such as listening, wisdom, discretion, or spiritual insight, that make them well suited for this role. Do they exhibit the fruit of love, joy, peace, forbearance, kindness, goodness, faithfulness, gentleness, and self-control? By engaging in this exercise, you can make a thoughtful decision regarding whom you can trust and confide in. Then, seek them out and practice confession.

# PRAYER FOCUS

Dear Lord, I seek Your guidance in selecting an individual to trust with my thoughts. Grant me the ability to identify someone who is compassionate, empathetic, and trustworthy. Give me the courage and strength to open up while also granting me the wisdom to gain knowledge from this experience. May this process bring me closer to finding healing, wholeness, and a stronger relationship with You. I pray in Jesus' name, Amen.

> *Recovery isn't a race. You don't have to feel guilty if it takes you longer than you thought it would.*
> *– Macklemore*

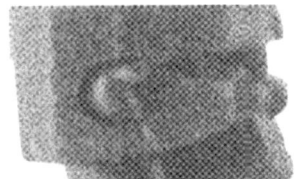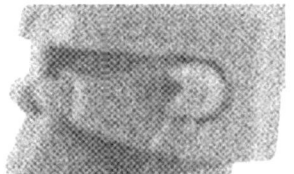

# DAY 20: CONFRONTING OUR FLAWS: STEP SIX

> *For I know that good itself does not dwell in me, that is, in my sinful nature. For I have the desire to do what is good, but I cannot carry it out.*
> *— Romans 7:18*

**STEP SIX: CONFRONT OUR FLAWS**

## REFLECTION

Every day, we are faced with a simple yet profound choice: do we live by the desires of the flesh or by the leading of the Spirit? Echoing the Apostle Paul, there's an inner conflict within us. What we nourish is what flourishes. By nurturing our spirit through grace, we mature and reflect on the fruits of the spirit: love, joy, peace, patience, kindness, goodness, faithfulness, gentleness, and self-control. When we grow in these areas, the flesh has to take a back seat. We no longer operate according to the ways of the world. When our heart is filled with God's love, it pushes out our sinful behaviors, making no room for them. Confessing our sins and flaws takes only one simple step: repenting and asking God, by His grace and mercy, to help remove them.

God will not override our free will but grants us the grace to combat the flesh.

Step Six is of great importance in the recovery journey, as it encourages us to examine our personal flaws, beyond simply pointing them out or acknowledging them. It entails a self-assessment, whereby we identify patterns of behavior, attitudes, or reactions that have had harmful or negative consequences in the past for ourselves and others. Step Six is not meant for self-condemnation; rather it aims to help us understand how these traits have impacted our well-being, relationships, and spiritual life. Armed with this understanding, we can take the necessary steps toward healing and personal growth.

When we look at Romans 7:18, we realize that a perpetual battle rages within each of us. On one hand, there exists a desire to do good and strive for transformation. On the other hand, our imperfections and weaknesses pull us in the opposite direction. It is crucial to remember that this struggle is something every individual faces in his or her own unique way. By confessing our limitations and recognizing the importance of seeking assistance, we can turn to God for guidance in overcoming our character flaws and cooperating with our transformation.

# DOING THE INNER WORK

Which of your negative habits and desires is the hardest to break?

How do you currently deal with your struggles? What helps you overcome them on your best days?

# PRAYER FOCUS

God, as I embark on Step Six of my journey toward recovery, I humbly seek clarity and honesty in recognizing the flaws within me. Please help me see myself through Your eyes, acknowledging both my imperfections and my potential for growth.

Grant me the wisdom to identify negative patterns in my behavior and the humility to admit to my shortcomings. I rely on Your guidance throughout this process of self-reflection, fully aware that it is by Your grace that true transformation and healing can take place within me.

Lord, grant me the courage to confront these truths about myself and the inner strength to become completely prepared for You to work within me. May this step bring me closer to becoming the person You have called me to be—someone who lives a life that mirrors Your love and goodness. In Jesus' name, I offer this prayer with gratitude. Amen.

> *You can either practice being right or practice being kind. — Anne Lamott*

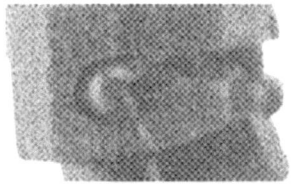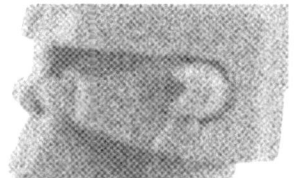

# DAY 21: INSIGHTFUL INTROSPECTION

> *I the LORD search the heart and examine the mind, to reward each person according to their conduct, according to what their deeds deserve.*
> *– Jeremiah 17:10*

## REFLECTION

Numerous articles discuss strategies for starting your day. Most of these are proactive tips and hacks aimed at boosting productivity and fitting in more work. There is nothing wrong with working smarter, but where does it end? Our culture places so much emphasis on productivity and dashing out of bed to be the early bird that we don't know how to end our day or to assess what truly matters in our day. We move from one situation, crisis, or project to another without taking a breath. We don't stop to smell the roses, so to speak. We can become so accustomed to auto-pilot and multitasking that we don't make the time to catch up with ourselves. So, while this is an uncommon question, it is equally important: how do you end your day?

Perhaps you feel you deserve to unwind by relaxing and watching Netflix, falling asleep on the couch, and repeating the cycle like Groundhog Day. How's that working out for you? The truth is, we should end our day in a way that prepares us for the next—and by that, I don't mean doing more work or thinking only about productivity. I mean putting away all distractions from the present moment and making some time for us to connect with God.

Take time in prayer, meditation, and introspection to process your day and feelings. Where did you see God at work? What areas in your heart and life need to be reset to fulfill God's desires for your life? It's essential to start the day well, but how you end it is significant too.

Today, we continue in Step Six on our journey of self-discovery. This step involves recognizing facets of our personality that could use work. As we've discussed, the process of noting our weaknesses isn't just about acknowledging them but assessing how they impact ourselves and those around us. This step instills humility and honesty, guiding us toward the transformation we seek. As you slow down your pace and move toward self-critique, be open and thorough, reflecting on both surface-level behaviors and underlying attitudes and motivations contributing to these character flaws.

Jeremiah 17:10 emphasizes that our innermost thoughts and emotions are always known to God. He says, "I the LORD search the heart and examine the mind." This means that we cannot do a thorough examination of ourselves through our own self-analysis. We have to humbly come before the Lord and ask the Holy Spirit to shine His searchlight in us to reveal our innermost thoughts and motivations. This is the only way to engage in honest and sincere self-reflection. As we contemplate this passage, let it inspire us to sincerely recognize our flaws while understanding that this self-awareness serves as a step toward genuine and enduring change.

## DOING THE INNER WORK

As you invite God to search your heart and examine your mind as in Jeremiah 17:10, what do you notice? What surface level behaviors need to change?

Dig a little deeper. What attitudes and motivations lie underneath your actions? You might start with the phrase "If I'm really honest ..." and then fill in how you feel and what you long for deep down.

What are those key character defects that feel glaring to you, as well as those buried under the surface?

# PRAYER FOCUS

Dear God, help me to list my character defects and see their impact on my life and on others. Grant me the humility and courage to confront them. Lead me through this process and prepare my heart for change. Help me to grow closer to You and become the person You want me to be. Amen.

> *Awareness is the greatest agent for change.*
> *– Eckhart Tolle*

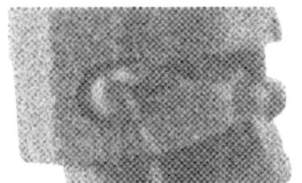 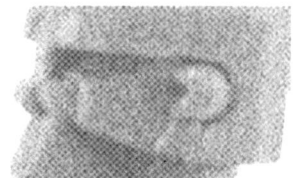

# DAY 22: PATH TO PURITY

* * * * * * * * * * * * * * * * * * * * * * * * * * * * * * * * * *

> *Therefore, since we have these promises, dear friends, let us purify ourselves from everything that contaminates body and spirit, perfecting holiness out of reverence for God.*
> *— 2 Corinthians 7:1*

## REFLECTION

Picking names for an unborn child can prove both fun and stressful all at once. That's because names, whether a family name or a biblical one, carry significance to a family. When we were expecting our first child, we gave her the same middle name as my wife and her mom: Katherine. When we looked into the meaning of the name, we found it means "pure." I know nowadays that the culture of purity, or the thought of it, gets a bad rap, but purity does not mean perfection. It is also not just about abstaining from sex outside of marriage. Purity means growing in God's intent and a God-given identity.

What if I told you that God wants to give you a new name? That name is not defined by your past, your current circumstances, or what the world thinks of you. God sent His only Son, Jesus, who paid the ultimate sacrifice for us to draw near to a holy God. When God sees us, He sees His sons and daughters covered by a mantle of holiness called "the breastplate of righteousness" (Ephesians 6:14). It is not a holiness we can earn or manufacture on our own; it is given to us by God with a sacrifice that has been bought and paid for.

As we reach the conclusion of Step Six today, think about the habits, thoughts, or behaviors that might be impeding your path toward holiness. Consider the situations, practices, and people that may trigger those impure thoughts, habits, or behaviors. Think of the joy of liberating yourself from these burdens and identify the steps you can take toward leading a purer and more devout life.

In 2 Corinthians 7:1, we are reminded of the importance of working toward purifying ourselves and embracing holiness. It urges us to reflect on ways to purify both our body and soul, making choices that honor our commitment to leading a recovering life.

## DOING THE INNER WORK

What are the habits, thoughts, or behaviors that might be impeding your path toward holiness?

In what ways do you need to invite God's grace into your life to allow holiness of heart and mind to take over?

# HEALING EXERCISE

Take some time for meditation and centering your thoughts. Envision yourself laying down your character flaws and impurities before God, one by one. Picture yourself emerging renewed, pure, and holy, fully prepared to embrace the changes essential for your recovery. After this meditation, jot down the actions you will take to cultivate holiness in both your body and soul. This written commitment can serve as a roadmap and reminder as you progress throughout your journey.

# PRAYER FOCUS

O God, I humbly ask for Your guidance in recognizing the flaws within me that I should overcome and the situations and practices I should steer away from. Give me the strength to keep my heart pure. Please lead me toward looking more like You. Show me the actions to purify my life, and enable me to live them out in word, deed, and thought. In the name of Jesus, Amen.

> *Sobriety was the greatest gift I ever gave myself.*
> *– Rob Lowe*

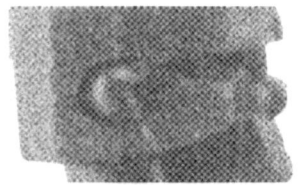 

# DAY 23: COMING WITH A BROKEN SPIRIT: STEP SEVEN

* * * * * * * * * * * * * * * * * * * * * * * * * * * * * * *

> *My sacrifice, O God, is a broken spirit; a broken and contrite heart you, God, will not despise.*
> **– Psalm 51:17**

**STEP SEVEN: PURSUE WISDOM**

## REFLECTION

Psalm 51 is a remarkable psalm because it is brutally honest. Here we have a proud and powerful leader like David being brought to his knees and confessing his *hidden* sin in tears to the Lord. David abused his power by forcing himself onto Bathsheba and had her husband Uriah sent to the battlefront where he was killed so that David could marry Bethsheba to cover up her pregnancy.

Pride and arrogance caused David to be blind to his sin and to pretend that everything was good on the outside when the inside was rotten. That pride hung over him for several months and hardened his heart to the truth. It took the prophet, Nathan, confronting him with his sin for David's eyes to be opened to his true condition. When the truth hit him, he fell on his face weeping and crying out to the Lord for forgiveness with a broken and contrite heart. It made him take ownership of his sin and face the consequences. That, my brothers and sisters, is true humility.

When we confess our sin, let us not do it in a superficial way but in all humility, ask the Lord to reveal the depths of our iniquity. Let that be a humbling experience before Him as we recognize how that sin has damaged our relationship with Him and hurt many other people down the line. Then we can truly repent and turn away from that sin, that bad habit, that selfishness, arrogance, and pride.

James the apostle reminds us,

*"But he gives us more grace". That is why scripture says: God opposes the proud but shows favor to the humble, submit yourselves, then, to God. Resist the devil, and he will flee from you. –James 4:6-7*

As we approach Day 23 and Step Seven, it's a time for further self-reflection. Throughout the scriptures, God constantly reminds us of the danger of pride and self-righteousness and the need seek Him with a humble and contrite heart. This step urges us to examine our flaws and truly comprehend and accept them. We should consider the qualities or actions that have hindered our progress, caused harm to others, or distanced us from the life we are called to lead.

Above all, we must be truthful with ourselves and with God and allow Him to expose the aspects of ourselves that require His grace and healing the most. The fact that God values a pure, honest, and humble heart underscores the power of humility and sincere repentance.

# DOING THE INNER WORK

Over the past several steps, you've named habits, actions, and attitudes you want to change. How have those patterns in your life impacted your choices, relationships with others, and relationship with God?

What secret sins and sinful roots has the Holy Spirit uncovered in you?

Can you see where pride and arrogance made you resistant to correction?

Even in relationships where another person has wronged you, can you humbly notice any area in which you might have had a role to play?

# PRAYER FOCUS

Heavenly Father. Please grant me the courage and transparency to seek Your truth to uncover every secret sin that I have not repented of due to my pride and self-righteousness. I recognize that You despise a proud heart, but a humble and contrite heart is very pleasing to You. I ask for the humble heart that will be open to truth about my sins and ugliness, even when it hurts, in Jesus' name. Amen.

> *Power is dangerous unless you have humility.*
> *– Richard J. Daley*

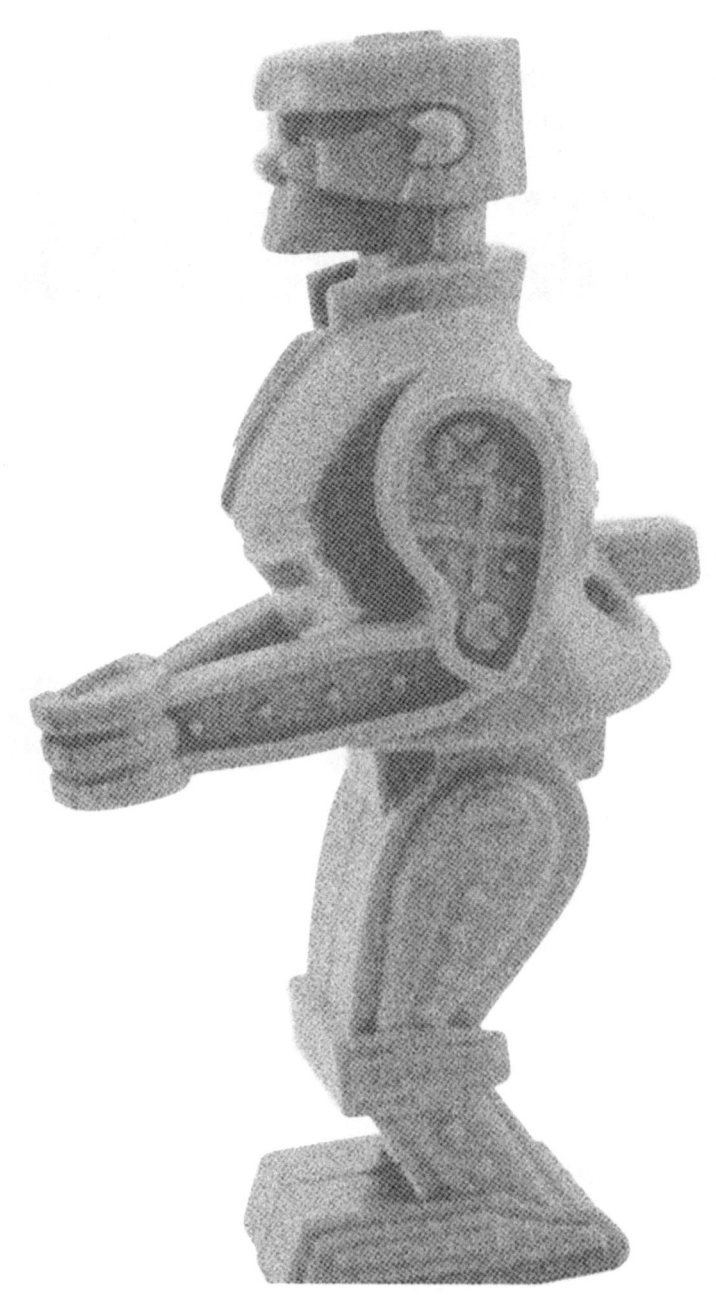

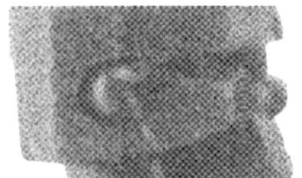 

# DAY 24: ASKING WITH HUMILITY

> *For those who exalt themselves will be humbled,*
> *and those who humble themselves will be exalted.*
> *– Mathew 23:12*

## REFLECTION

When my kids ask for something in a demanding tone, skipping the "please" and "thank you," it feels like an order rather than a request. Naturally, as a parent, this doesn't sit well. I usually ask them to try again, emphasizing manners, as I want them to communicate respectfully with everyone. As I correct my kids, I can't help but think about how we sometimes come to God with a similar posture.

Often, we approach God with a laundry list of demands, as if God were a cosmic vending machine. Instead, we are taught repeatedly to come to God with a right heart—a humble heart. We are not to be afraid to ask God for what we need, and yes, even at times, what we want. Whatever the request, however, there is a way to talk to God: in a manner of humility.

As we journey through Step Seven, we can begin to grasp the significance of humility in our growth. Humility means recognizing and embracing our limitations and understanding our reliance on God's guidance and strength. In recovery, humility becomes crucial when we seek help to overcome our weaknesses. Take a moment to ponder the essence of humility in your life. How does admitting your limitations, vulnerabilities, insecurities, and dependence on God's grace elevate you spiritually? Reflect on the power of humility—how it shifts your perspective from self-reliance to God-reliance, from the stiffness of pride to the malleability of change, and from isolation to forming a connection with Jesus.

Humility invites us to shed the layers of ego and pride that often blind us to ourselves. It allows us to stand before God with honesty without any façade or cover-up of our imperfections, eagerly seeking His grace. Remember that humility is not about demeaning ourselves but about recognizing our need for God. After all, humility is a trait that the devil cannot possess.

Humility is a paradox. It is fascinating how spiritual growth and elevation stem from a place of bowing down. Matthew 23:12 reminds us of this truth: the first will be last and the last will be first. Those who lower themselves in humility will be lifted up; those who hold themselves in high regard will be let down. Embrace humility today!

# DOING THE INNER WORK

How does humility shift your posture before God?

What do you have to lose and what have you to gain when you put on humility in your journey?

Take a moment to ask God's forgiveness for when you've acted from a place of pride and humbly ask God for what you really need deep down.

## PRAYER FOCUS

Almighty God, I come before You with a heart seeking true humility as I reflect on my life. Please guide me to understand the importance of humility as a means to grow spiritually and help me recognize that acknowledging my limitations brings me closer to You. I need Your help in over-coming my flaws. May this newfound humility strengthen my connection with You. In Jesus' name, Amen.

> *You can't have a drug problem for 30 years and then expect to have it be solved in 28 days.*
> *– Matthew Perry*

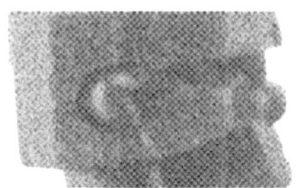

# DAY 25: SEEKING WISDOM ON THE PATH

*Plans are established by seeking advice;*
*so if you wage war, obtain guidance.*
*– Proverbs 20:18*

## REFLECTION

Countless self-help books, podcasts, and gurus like Dr. Phil and Oprah are eager to offer guidance in our lives, contributing to one of the largest industries globally. People who often feel adrift come to them seeking direction. Where do you turn for advice? In tough situations, reaching out to a friend or seeking counsel is often our instinctive response. Godly counsel is essential, but if you go to people who do not operate in God's wisdom, something major will always be lacking. So, where do we go for direction?

Years ago, when I was starting to drive, I remember having to print out MapQuest directions—yes, complex copy directions—to navigate my way on a trip. Before GPS, people used a map! Today, we can quickly go to an app on our mobile device to guide our direction. As an added bonus, these apps are updated regularly for new routes and accuracy and can guide us around traffic. We place our trust in a device that will lead us along the way, but even the most empowered app will occasionally let us down. If you want direction for your life, there is only one go-to with 100% precision and accuracy. God gives us wisdom through the scriptures, such as prayer, godly counsel, and a whole host of other ways, when we intentionally seek Him.

On this day, as we continue in Step Seven, we must begin by appreciating the value of seeking guidance and shared wisdom in our journey toward transformation. Let's pause for a moment and reflect on how the advice we receive from others can help us overcome our weaknesses. Our path is not a solitary one. It becomes enriched by the insights and experiences of those around us. After all, no man is an island. Human beings are designed to be social creatures. How does the wisdom of a mentor, the understanding of a leader, or the support of a friend contribute to our commitment to self-improvement? By listening to others, we can gain advice, moral support, and encouragement. Seeking guidance is a sign of our strength in embracing vulnerability and recognizing the power of wisdom in our growth.

As you meditate today, consider how sharing your intentions with someone you trust can provide insights into your challenges. It's essential to remember that seeking advice is not a sign of weakness but a humble acknowledgment of our need for support and an active step toward recovery. By broadening our understanding in listening to the perspectives of another, we strengthen our dedication to change and continue progressing on our path toward growth.

Proverbs 20:18 highlights the significance of seeking advice and being prepared. Take a moment to reflect on the meaning behind this verse. How can we leverage the wisdom of others to enhance our lives? When we encounter obstacles, seeking advice from others can be immensely valuable.

Their distinctive perspectives and insights can guide us in navigating challenges in ways that ultimately lead to triumph. The wisdom and support of wise counselors might be exactly what we need to overcome hurdles and emerge victorious in the end.

# DOING THE INNER WORK

In what areas of your life do you need God's direction?

How can you make it a daily practice to ask God for direction?

# HEALING EXERCISE

It's always a good idea to seek guidance and counsel from someone you trust before embarking on a journey. It requires humbly admitting you don't have all of the answers. Consider reaching out to someone with experience or whose perspectives you highly regard and engage in conversation. Later, take a moment to note the insights and advice you've received. Reflect on how you can incorporate this wisdom into your strategy for overcoming any challenges you might face. Maintaining a written record of this shared knowledge will serve as a resource and constant reminder of the guidance that supports you along your journey.

# CLOSING PRAYER

Heavenly Father, grant me the humility to seek guidance and the openness to receive and apply the wisdom offered by those You have placed in my life. Bless my conversations and reflections with clarity and insight. Help me to integrate the valuable perspectives of others into my journey toward growth. May their wisdom complement Your guidance toward greater understanding and effective action. In Jesus' name, Amen.

> *You should never try to be better than someone else,*
> *you should always be learning from others.*
> *– John Wooden*

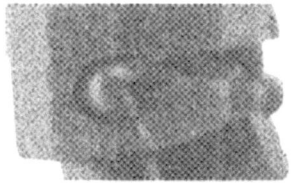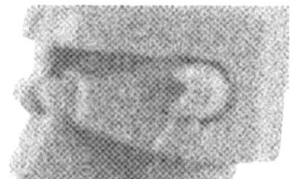

# DAY 26: ADVOCACY AND HEALING: STEP EIGHT

*Speak up for those who cannot speak for themselves, for the rights of all who are destitute. Speak up and judge fairly; defend the rights of the poor and needy.*
*– Proverbs 31:8-9*

## STEP EIGHT: SEEK PEACE

# REFLECTION

When we acknowledge our shortcomings, it is easy to focus on how our behaviors have affected us. But what about those who've suffered due to our choices? Healing isn't an isolated journey. What if God's healing extends to all affected by our actions? Sometimes, we heal in isolation apart from those people, and other times, we heal together in a community.

Step Eight takes us deeper than thinking of ourselves and invites us to a door we don't often knock on. We must acknowledge the people of our past and present that we have harmed. This Step can be daunting due to the fear it evokes. It places us in a position of vulnerability rather than control. It involves listing the wrongs committed, and the individuals directly or indirectly impacted by those wrongs. The time to shift the blame is over. We must take the time to write down those names and recall those situations as best as possible to confess our faults. It's time to clean up our side of the street. This step needs to be approached prayerfully and wisely, so that we do not cause further harm to ourselves and others. We advocate for our healing, as we acknowledge the hurt we've caused.

That is why, when moving forward to Step Eight, it becomes necessary for us to expand our understanding of the concept of harm. We must consider not just the harm we may have caused individuals but the more subtle forms of harm that exist within our society. Today's reflection prompts us to contemplate how those who lack a voice or power experience harm. It is important for us to recognize how silence or inaction can exacerbate the harm. We pause to consider our role in advocating for marginalized individuals and those in poverty. This step goes beyond admitting mistakes. It involves understanding our place within these dynamics. We ought to question how our actions or inaction might have harmed those unable to speak for themselves. It's crucial to examine how we can stand up as advocates for justice and fairness.

Proverbs 31:8-9 challenges us to stand up for those who are often marginalized and unheard. Let's reflect on the ways we can utilize our resources, voice, and influence to make an impact on our communities and support those in need. We need to give a voice to the voiceless. This passage also encourages us to broaden our perspective when seeking reconciliation by focusing not only on those closest to us but also addressing any damage we may have caused society as a whole.

We are urged to act and work toward building a world that benefits everyone.

# DOING THE INNER WORK

Take a moment to start your list. Who have you harmed by your actions or inaction? Start closest with family and friends, moving out to coworkers, neighbors, others in your community, and ultimately, the world.

As you look at your list, what emotions stir up within you? Any that surprise you?

Take a moment to surrender each name to the Lord and receive God's grace and forgiveness.

In what instances might the wrong approach cause further harm to ourselves and others?

# PRAYER FOCUS

Lord, guide me in Step Eight to see the harm I've caused directly and indirectly, the harm I am aware of and the harm I am not aware of. Please help me understand how I may have affected those who cannot defend themselves. Give me the strength to advocate for the marginalized and to seek justice and healing. Guide me in acknowledging with a willing heart my societal role and creating a list of those

I've harmed to make amends. Let my recovery be a journey of compassion in line with Your call to support the vulnerable. Amen.

> *Injustice anywhere is a threat to justice everywhere.*
> *– Martin Luther King, Jr.*

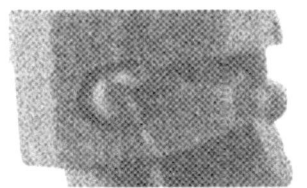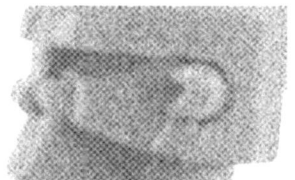

# DAY 27: SEEKING PEACE IN RELATIONSHIPS

*If it is possible, as far as it depends on you,*
*live at peace with everyone.*
*— Romans 12:18*

## REFLECTION

We can't alter the past, the actions of others, or our own past deeds. Nonetheless, God grants us the power through our free will to enact change in the present. It means doing the next right thing, which presents us with an opportunity to keep our side of the street clean. Our peace is not dependent on how others respond to us, but it is dependent on God and how we respond to adversity. When we do the next right thing in the eyes of God and respond to situations God's way, the outcome will be better than if we were operating on our own volition.

Our response to others can be a predictor of the outcome. We cannot seek, speak, or live in peace without self-control. But when our hearts are filled with God's love and wisdom, we will surprise ourselves with how we deal with situations. What relationship do you need peace in right now? The challenge for all of us is to surrender that person and situation to God and know that God can bring peace where it may not seem possible.

As we progress with Step Eight, it's important to dedicate some time to self-reflection regarding our relationships. This means creating a list of individuals who have been part of your life, past and present, and contemplating the nature of each relationship. These connections may include friends, family members, colleagues, or even acquaintances. Evaluate how these relationships have changed over time and recognize the dynamics involved. Consider the mutual impact of each party involved. This process isn't about judging others but about gaining insight into your interactions. Reflect on any harm, misunderstandings needing resolution, or relationships needing healing. By conducting this inventory, you'll be able to recognize your role in these relationships and prepare yourself for making amends where necessary.

Romans 12:18 speaks of the importance of our responsibility in fostering harmonious interactions within all our relationships, while acknowledging that we cannot control how others behave or respond. Reflecting on this verse urges me to ponder how I can embody this principle in my relationships.

# DOING THE INNER WORK

Which relationships are most important to you? List the names of those individuals and groups.

Which relationships need adjustments to be healthier? What changes—some big, others little—do you sense God leading you to make in those relationships to improve them?

# PRAYER FOCUS

Heavenly Father, guide me as I review my relationships. Help me seek peace and resolution, humbly acknowledging my role in any discord and courageously pursuing making amends. May Your love and grace lead me to healing, clarity, and reconciliation in all my interactions. Let my actions strive for peace with all, reflecting Romans 12:18. Guide me in empathy and harmony with Your love. In Jesus' name, Amen.

> *Acceptance doesn't mean resignation; it means understanding that something is what it is and there's got to be a way through it. — Michael J. Fox*

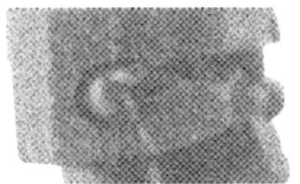

# DAY 28: EMBRACING A NEW PATH

> *Enter through the narrow gate. For wide is the gate and broad is the road that leads to destruction, and many enter through it. But small is the gate and narrow the road that leads to life, and only a few find it.*
> *– Matthew 7:13-14*

## REFLECTION

When we pursue God's path, we find it's narrow and less traveled. Few opt for it. The easy route—the world's way—is wide and open. This is the path of least resistance. Daily, we confront the choice of which path to take. It means something significant. Consider the wide road we previously went down that did not lead us anywhere fruitful. It led us to a place of hurt that we inflicted on ourselves and others.

By contrast, the new path He is leading you to is one of adventure. It can be terrifying when we do not know all the twists and turns. The good news is that we are not alone. God becomes our Guide, and when we join the community of faith, that community will also support us along our journey. We grow and walk into our God-identity when we step out of our comfort zone. Our daily check-ins with our Guide will direct our steps. And God will not let us wander directionless. When we get off course and feel lost, God will always be there to redirect our steps.

Assuming responsibility for our errors and transgressions while actively striving to separate ourselves from these past actions is important. It's necessary to recognize all the points at which we have deviated from the right path and then make a deliberate decision to alter our trajectory. By creating space between us and our past deeds, we can maintain our covenant with God to be on a new journey.

One of the sayings that has become proverbial wisdom in recovery circles is not associating with the "people, places, and things" that take you down the wrong path. In Matthew 7, Jesus describes a similar path as a broad one that is easy to take but leads to destruction. Following Jesus down the narrow path will mean making earthly sacrifices for eternal rewards.

As you contemplate this scripture, think about how you can distance yourself from close relationships as well as behaviors that have been detrimental or contrary to your values and God's Word. How can you honor God by wholeheartedly committing to following His will on your journey toward recovery?

# DOING THE INNER WORK

How, if at all, have old people, places, or things led you down a "broad" path as Jesus described in Matthew 7?

Who and what are the people, places, and things that help cultivate your journey down the narrow path?

# HEALING EXERCISE

Write down the types of qualities you want to have in your family, in your relationships, and in your friendships from your present and future. Of course, we all have regrets, but now is the time for a fresh start. Take that list of friends and behaviors that you want to have in your life and boldly ask God to give them to you. Reflect on those individuals who are further ahead in their recovery and who are living out those qualities. Invite them to coffee or tea and spend some time with them, asking how they have taken the narrow path in their own lives.

# PRAYER FOCUS

Heavenly Father, guide me as I accept responsibility for my past and seek to change. Grant me the wisdom and courage to move away from harmful past behaviors and relationships and reorientate my actions to Your values and will. May my commitment to transformation be evident in my daily life, reflecting Your love and grace. In Jesus' name, Amen.

> *When we are no longer able to change a situation, we are challenged to change ourselves.*
> *— Viktor E. Frankl*

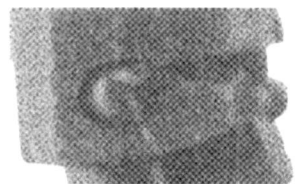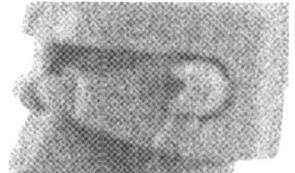

# DAY 29: PRIORITIZING AMENDS IN STEP NINE

*But Zacchaeus stood up and said to the Lord, "Look, Lord! Here and now I give half of my possessions to the poor, and if I have cheated anybody out of anything, I will pay back four times the amount."*
*– Luke 19:8*

**STEP NINE: MAKE AMENDS**

## REFLECTION

The only way to experience healing is through our confession, but confession without repentance and the desire for reconciliation is only lip service. Our words carry only so far if the action does not accompany it. Otherwise, we become repeat offenders.

The word for repentance in the Greek is *metanoia*. For the longest time, scholars suggested that *metanoia* only meant a change of direction: "a 180-degree turn." But the Greek captures more: "a change of mind." Working the steps is not simply behavior modification; it is asking God to rewire our thinking. When we choose to adopt the mind of Christ, we begin to think and act like Jesus. We begin to see the world and the people around us with new eyes. We recalibrate our thinking to the mind of Christ (1 Corinthians 2:16).

The Ninth Step is a tough one that requires us to confront our past actions and those whom we have harmed. This requires courage and could feel overwhelming in certain situations. This step involves two difficult acts. The first is asking for forgiveness from others, knowing the grace and freedom that comes through heartfelt repentance. We can't control the responses of others, but as God leads us to do the right thing, we trust that we have His favor, for "When a man's ways please the LORD, He makes even his enemies to be at peace with him" (Proverbs 16:7 NKJV).

The second thing to do is to make amends. That means to compensate or make up for a wrongdoing to the best of our ability. This is not a legal requirement. It stems more from natural justice and the fruit of a truly repentant heart. In making this decision, it is more important than ever to lean on God for strength and surround ourselves with godly people to support us in our quest.

You may remember the story of Zacchaeus in Luke 19:1-10 from Sunday school. This was about a tax collector, who came from a despised class, seen to be in league with the Roman authorities, as well as lining their own pockets with the surplus. So here was tiny Zacchaeus perched on a tree to get a glimpse of Jesus preaching to the crowd. To his surprise, Jesus sees him and calls him out by name and then announces He is going to stay with him that day. Zacchaeus is so touched by the love and acceptance of the Lord that he is moved to repentance. But watch this. He offers to give half of his possessions to the poor and restore fourfold all that he has unjustly taken. No one told him to do that. It came from a deep conviction and the grace of God upon his life.

Admitting our mistakes, apologizing, and trying to make amends can lead to greater forgiveness and reconciliation than we could ever fathom. As you meditate on this passage, imagine how you will make restitution with the ones you've wronged. Remember to confess your mistakes and approach them with honesty and humility!

## DOING THE INNER WORK

Who from your Step Eight list do you sense God leading you to approach first to make amends?

Who will be praying for you, supporting you, and encouraging you as you go through the process of making amends? Reach out to those companions today, if you haven't already.

How are you honestly feeling about the process of making amends? Name your emotions and put them before the Lord.

How will you respond if the other party refuses to accept your apology or your offer of restitution?

## PRAYER FOCUS

Dear Jesus, as I set out to correct my past mistakes, grant me Your discernment. Assist me in approaching those to whom I've caused pain with a humble posture seeking forgiveness and reconciliation. May the manner in which I conduct myself echo the lessons learned from the story of Zacchaeus, discovering mercy on my path toward reconciliation and restitution concerning those whom I have harmed. In Jesus' name, Amen.

> *Courageous people do not fear forgiving, for the sake of peace. – Nelson Mandela*

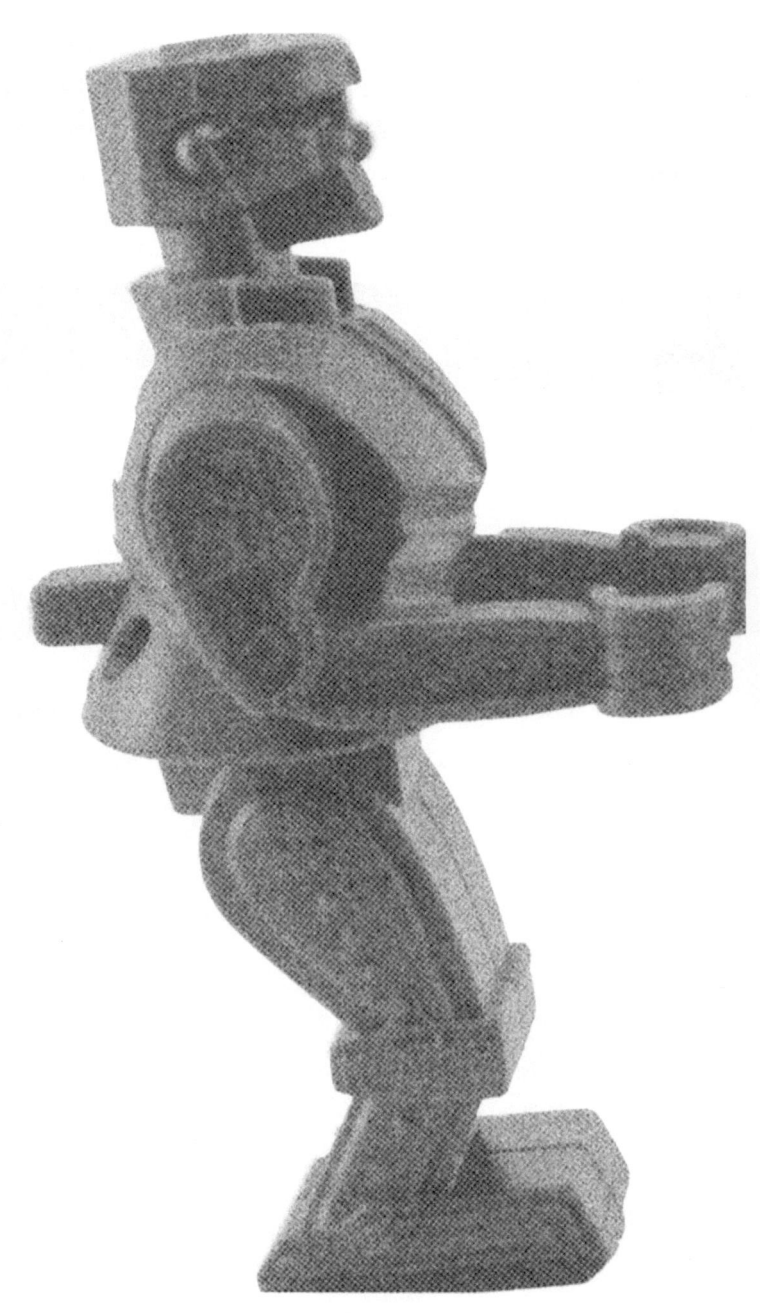

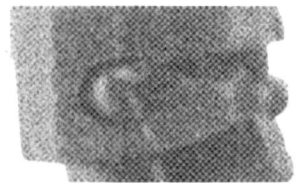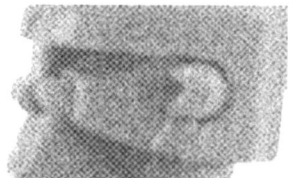

# DAY 30: PREPARING
# FOR DIFFICULT
# CONVERSATIONS

> *The words of the reckless pierce like swords,*
> *but the tongue of the wise brings healing.*
> *— Proverbs 12:18*

## REFLECTION

Many have heard of the Boy Scout motto: "Be prepared."
As a pastor and public speaker, I hold preaching, speaking,
and teaching in high regard. Being unprepared is a night-
mare scenario for me, as it not only dishonors God but also
leads to embarrassment and a loss of morale among the
congregation. After all, they expect me to have some level
of preparation, expertise, and insight—and if I fail them, I
fail God too. I have learned that my preparation is critical,
but what I have prepared to say is only part of it. I also must
prepare by getting my heart and mind attuned to God.

The first part anyone can learn in a preaching or public
speaking class. The latter is not formally taught but caught
along the way. I apply this same concept when I gear up for

difficult conversations. These days, I do not rehearse what I will say, but I try to tune my spirit with God's Spirit. The thing is, I can be well prepared in the worldly sense, but things can go wrong. The outcome of difficult conversations becomes significantly better, and often miraculous, when I am prayerfully taking the situation to God. Though I cannot control or dictate what the other person will say or how that person will respond, I can be at peace with God, knowing I put Him first.

As you gear up for the rigorous dialogue involved in the act of reconciliation, it is crucial to be mindful of the power and influence your words can wield. We know the tongue can be a weapon of destruction or it can be a balm of healing. Your utterances can either mend or inflict damage; hence, conducting these discussions with awareness and sensitivity is essential. Consider your past conversations. Were your words comforting or intimidating? Think about how you could use language to sincerely express your respect, showing you understand the distress caused and committing to making things right.

Employing *active* listening skills during such interactions is vital for a deeper conversation and empathy toward the sentiments and viewpoints of those affected by your actions. This means we don't interject all the time. Instead, we stay quiet and allow others to share their thoughts and feelings. Bear in mind that our demeanor throughout this discourse can considerably affect not only our healing process but also that of those whom we've wronged. The potency and repercussions of verbal expressions cannot be understated. Proverbs 12:18 offers valuable counsel in this matter, urging us to select our words judiciously so as to promote recovery and understanding within the situation.

# DOING THE INNER WORK

Take some time to prepare your heart and mind. Center your thoughts on God's love, peace, and forgiveness in your own life. Offer an honest prayer to God as you name your emotions and ask for God's peace and guidance.

Now, take some time to pray for the other person. Pray for their healing and openness and that God would be with them in the conversation as well.

Sit quietly asking and listening to God for any wisdom regarding what to say and how to say it. Write down anything you hear or notice. It might even be an indication of the right time. If you aren't sure whether it's God or your own fears speaking, tune your ears to hear His voice. If you are still uncertain, ask God to make it clear.

## PRAYER FOCUS

Lord, as I prepare for these conversations, guide my words and help me to listen. Help me to speak with honesty, empathy, and wisdom, bringing healing through my sincere efforts to make amends. Amen.

> *Most people do not listen with the intent to under-*
> *stand; they listen with the intent to reply.*
> *– Stephen Covey*

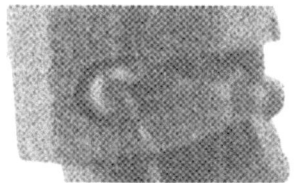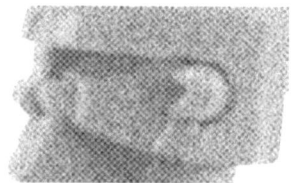

# DAY 31: REFLECTING ON THE IMPACT OF AMENDS

*Above all, love each other deeply, because love covers over a multitude of sins.*
*– 1 Peter 4:8*

## REFLECTION

God can and will forgive us of our sins, but we have no control over whether people will forgive us here on earth. This can be difficult to imagine, but it is part of the reality of our own frailties and the degree of wrong done to a person. Not everyone will accept our amends, no matter how sincerely we make them. Even if they are generous enough to do so, it does not mean that the relationship will be restored to its past form. A divorced couple, for example, can forgive one another, negotiate, and have a cordial relationship but not necessarily remarry or remain in the same relationship dynamic.

In these conversations, we must do three things: check our expectations at the door, invite God in, and stay realistically hopeful. There are also certainly times when it is not appropriate to have a conversation, as it might cause harm to ourselves and others. This can happen when emotions are running too high, the other person is not ready, when we are feeling unsafe, or when past trauma can be triggered. In such instances, writing a letter that you may never send and seeking a spiritual guide who can pray with you or envisioning speaking to that person with Jesus present can also contribute to healing. No matter the result, the transformative work God intends within you as you pursue amends will be remarkable.

The importance of preparing and reflecting on your journey's impact cannot be overstated. A mere apology falls short, but impactful action can reshape your relationships and offer both parties a profound sense of peace and serenity. After the conversation, pause for a moment to contemplate how these dialogues have emotionally and spiritually impacted you. Did they provide relief, aid in opening new insights, or possibly reopen old wounds?

1 Peter 4:8 invites us to, above all else, love. Opting to act out of love and love alone has granted me the ability to steer my way in challenging situations, acting in forgiveness and reconciliation. Acting in love isn't always straightforward. It demands commitment and continuous effort, but it is essential.

# DOING THE INNER WORK

When we are entering the process of making amends how can we:

Check our expectations at the door?

Invite God into the situation?

Stay realistically hopeful?

# HEALING EXERCISE

This exercise requires you to journal about the emotions and insights that have surfaced post making amends. Journaling doesn't have to mean writing lengthy or time-consuming entries. Write down as many words as you feel are necessary to express your thoughts and feelings. Consider sharing these reflections with someone you trust, recognizing the intricate mix of emotions involved in repairing relationships and the continual journey of forgiveness and reconciliation. By sharing these thoughts, you not only gain clarity for yourself but also open the door for deeper insights and support from someone who understands and cares about your growth. Take some time to do this now.

# PRAYER FOCUS

Heavenly Father, thank You for guiding me through my amends. Help me to continue reflecting on these experiences, nurturing the relationships that have been healed and living a life marked by love and forgiveness. Amen.

> *Forgiveness is a strange thing. It can sometimes be easier to forgive our enemies than our friends. It can be hardest of all to forgive people we love.*
> *– Fred Rogers*

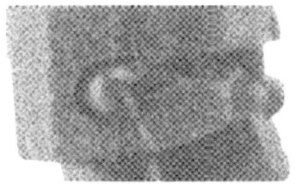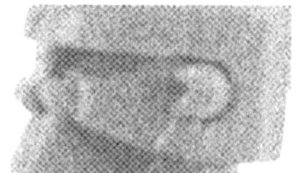

# DAY 32: EMBRACING DAILY REFLECTION: STEP TEN

*Let us examine our ways and test them,*
*and let us return to the LORD.*
*— Lamentations 3:40*

**STEP TEN: EMBRACE DAILY REFLECTION**

## REFLECTION

Any construction builder will tell you that a firm, strong, and level foundation is key to the entire structure. The 12 Steps each build on one another and may seem repetitive, but checking and double-checking our work ensures we achieve our goals. Daily reflections may appear redundant on the surface, yet they hold essential value and yield rewards at a deeper level. The chaos of our unmanaged lives didn't happen overnight, and healing clarity won't occur in an instant. It's a lifelong journey, walking every step with Jesus.

These Steps are available to all who are willing to embark on this path, especially taking a personal moral inventory. While there will be detours, the steps remind us that we cannot do this alone. Recovery is not easy and takes work. However, working these steps will build a foundation for life that will never crumble, no matter the outside conditions or disasters in the natural world.

Recovery, like the Christian life, is not about the destination but the process. It is not about getting into Heaven but getting a little bit of Heaven into us, as reflected in the Lord's Prayer: that we see God's will done on earth as it is in Heaven. In recovery, we will slip and fall, perhaps not necessarily a relapse of substance abuse but in our way of thinking, processing, and doing everyday life. My friends, it's about progress not perfection.

# DOING THE INNER WORK

What rhythms help you the most in your personal journey with the Lord?

Remembering it's often the little changes that add up over time, what are your habits of reflection for this season?

When and where will you practice reflection? Who can hold you accountable as you establish these habits?

As you reflect on your personal moral inventory today, what sins do you need to confess to God and where do you need to make amends?

## PRAYER FOCUS

Lord, guide me in my daily reflection, granting me the insight to recognize my strengths and the areas in my life that need improvement. Help me to apply this daily reflection for continual growth and alignment with Your will. Amen.

> *Reflective thinking turns experience into insight.*
> *— John Maxwell*

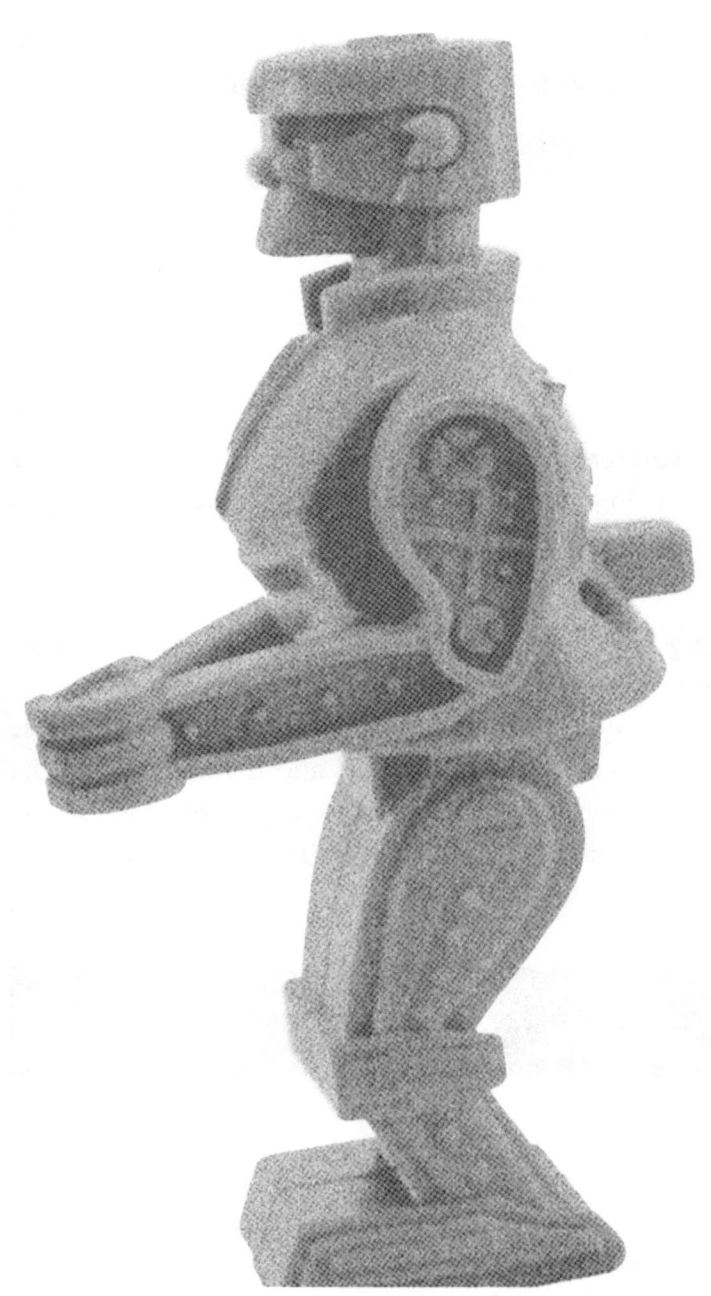

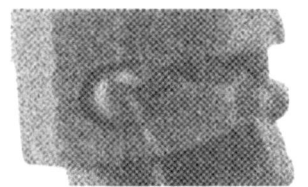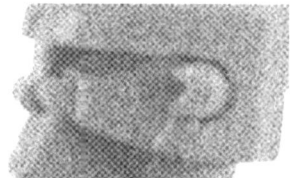

# DAY 33: AWARENESS OF TRIGGERS

> *So, if you think you are standing firm, be careful
> that you don't fall! No temptation has overtaken
> you except what is common to mankind.*
> *– 1 Corinthians 10:12-13*

## REFLECTION

Any addict will tell you they are only one bad decision away from a relapse. In faith terms, we call this "temptation." After a relapse and subsequent period of sobriety, individuals often reflect on where they erred and the triggers that led to their relapse. The acronym H.A.L.T. (Hungry, Angry, Lonely, Tired), stating four of the most common stressors in recovery, has become a go-to for many to prevent a regrettable decision. When experiencing any of those conditions, we can make a fatal decision. All of us are one decision away from destroying our progress and position in life. Understanding and acknowledging this simple fact is a sobering reality that can help us stay humble. It keeps us from putting ourselves on a pedestal and helps us remain conscious of the enemy to our souls who wants to take us out.

Have you paused to analyze your triggers? Recognizing and addressing our subconscious triggers plays a pivotal role in the journey of healing. Understanding the external and internal cues that might hinder your progress and reflecting on the situations, emotions, or people that trigger you allows you to create effective coping strategies. This heightened awareness gives you the power to actively avoid potential setbacks or relapses and make intentional, healthy choices that support your long-term recovery and overall well-being.

# DOING THE INNER WORK

What are your triggers? What situations or circumstances tend to bring out the aspects of your old self that you wish to shed?

What is your game plan? What will you do to avoid or lessen the temptation of those triggers?

# PRAYER FOCUS

Almighty God, enlighten me. Help me identify my triggers and equip me with the strength to manage them. Keep me steadfast on my path of recovery. Amen.

> *Not everything that is faced can be changed, but nothing can be changed until it is faced.*
> *– James Baldwin*

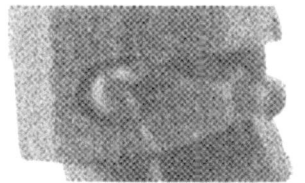 

# DAY 34: CULTIVATING GRATITUDE

> *Give thanks in all circumstances;*
> *for this is God's will for you in Christ Jesus.*
> *– 1 Thessalonians 5:18*

## REFLECTION

One of our family practices to build gratitude is to ask everyone around the dinner table what they are thankful for today. By doing so, we hope to instill a sense of gratitude in small ways in our kids while they are still young. It's remarkable how sharing or jotting down our gratitude can lift us, even when we feel low.

Science has proven that practicing gratitude can benefit us in many ways. These include enhanced mental health, improved physical health, better sleep, more empathy, less aggression, stronger relationships, improved self-esteem, and living with a "glass-half-full" attitude.

Gratitude takes the focus off of us and puts it squarely on God. In all the staff and board meetings I facilitate, it has become a practice to share how we see God at work and what we are grateful for. I also start this practice with guys in recovery who I spiritually mentor. It's incredible how straightforward gratitude practice can transform the mood and dynamics of a room.

Incorporating gratitude into our daily lives can profoundly influence overall wellness. This is a major one, but it is often overlooked. Taking the time to acknowledge and appreciate the blessings in your life can transition your mindset from pessimism to optimism and from lack to plenty. This shift nurtures a heightened satisfaction and joy across various areas of life. Appreciation spreads with a ripple effect, positively influencing every sphere of your life.

Consider this: everything you have, whether it's good health, a job you love, a caring family, and a comfortable home, can vanish instantly. This isn't meant to frighten you but to remind you of life's uncertainties. We never truly know what's coming next, so it's important to count it all as joy every day for the people and things we're blessed with.

To fully understand the importance of thankfulness in all of life's dimensions, it is crucial to contemplate sincerely what 1 Thessalonians 5:18 challenges us to do. We unlock gratitude's power during our path toward recovery. Through the regular practice of expressing appreciation, we develop a grateful spirit that permits us to find comfort even amidst strenuous situations.

## DOING THE INNER WORK

How can you begin to cultivate a daily practice of gratitude?

Establish a gratitude list right now. What are the top 10 things you are giving thanks to God for?

# HEALING EXERCISE

Starting a journal dedicated to expressing gratitude can be an effective strategy for nurturing a positive frame of mind and putting on the mind of Christ. Start small but start somewhere. It could be the first sip of your morning coffee, a breath of fresh air, or your baby's smile. This uncomplicated practice can transform your day. Spend some time now listing the things you are grateful for, either in a journal or the space below.

# PRAYER FOCUS

Dear God, You are the Creator and Sustainer of the entire universe! Fill my heart with gratitude. Let this practice enhance my recovery, bringing joy, peace, and a deeper appreciation of Your blessings. Amen.

> *Gratitude is the ability to experience life as a gift. It liberates us from the prison of self-preoccupation.*
> *— John Ortberg*

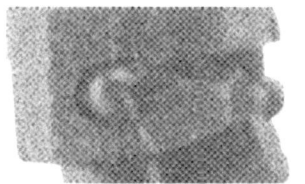

# DAY 35: EXPLORING YOUR UNDERSTANDING OF PRAYER: STEP ELEVEN

> *Do not be anxious about anything, but in everything by prayer and supplication with thanksgiving let your requests be made known to God.*
> *— Philippians 4:6 (ESV)*

### STEP ELEVEN: SEEK GOD'S WILL DAILY

## REFLECTION

In any relationship, the better we communicate, make ourselves available, and involve our entire selves, the stronger that relationship becomes. In Christian terms, we call this God's sanctifying love and grace. It involves growing in God's love and grace and recognizing that God is never done with us until we meet God face to face. It's a lifelong process, not a fire insurance or get-out-of-hell-free card.

We can cultivate an authentic relationship with God in many ways. One way is by embracing the gift of prayer. As we grow in prayer, our hearts and lives will change even though our outward circumstances may not.

Prayer looks different for everyone. My wife Callie wakes up early and journals in prayer. I like having more consecrated time at night and pray as I make commutes in the car throughout the day, picking up and dropping off my kids. Some like to walk in nature where they see God's magnificence all around them, while others find a favorite chair and quiet place in their home. Regardless of your method, take on the Nike motto and *"Just Do It."* Your style and methodology will change over time, and not getting into a rut is critical. Allow your time with God to be a continuous conversation. Go on a date with God to your favorite spot or wherever you are directed. It is not about quantity, but consistent quality. If you find yourself repeating the same prayer every single day until you sound like a broken record, take the time to switch things up.

The Eleventh Step entails the development of a profound and more intimate relationship with one's Higher Power, specifically Jesus, through prayer. This practice goes beyond simply reciting words. It involves an ongoing conversation that encourages introspection and contemplation. Through this process of self-discovery, individuals can assess how prayer functions in their own lives—whether it acts as a beacon of comfort during difficult times, a channel for seeking wisdom in the midst of dilemmas or uncertainties, or a means to express appreciation for life's gifts. Developing a more profound and meaningful prayer life can and will give you daily strength and clarity!

Philippians 4:6 tells us to pursue God in prayer while openly expressing our concerns, hopes, and expressions of gratitude. Prayer strengthens our relationship with God, so we begin to understand and pursue God's will for our lives over our own. Prayer is surrendering our control over to the care of God since God will do for us what we cannot do for ourselves.

## DOING THE INNER WORK

In what ways do you need God's help today? Where in your life are you anxious? Take a moment to honestly lift those people and circumstances to God with thanksgiving.

Prayer is a two-way conversation. After you pray, sit for a moment in the silence listening. Jot down anything you notice or hear. It might be a word or words, a scripture verse, an image, or simply how you feel. The more you practice listening to God, the easier it becomes to pick up God's still, small voice.

# PRAYER FOCUS

Eternal God, help me deepen my understanding and practice of prayer. May it be a bridge between my heart and Yours. I want to be honest with You by expressing my deepest needs and receive Your peace in my soul. Grant me the wisdom to find You in both silence and spoken words. Amen.

> *Our prayers may be awkward. Our attempts may be feeble. But since the power of prayer is in the one who hears it and not in the one who says it, our prayers do make a difference. – Max Lucado*

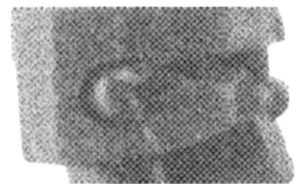 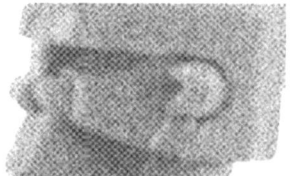

# DAY 36: THE ROLE OF MEDITATION

*Be still, and know that I am God ...*
*– Psalm 46:10*

## REFLECTION

The older I get, the harder it is to have tolerance for people who are always talking and never listening. This may sound harsh, but a reputation begins to precede them when this becomes their prime communication style. People avoid them and are afraid of getting trapped in long conversations. This is due to a lack of self-awareness—an invaluable trait to cultivate in our lives. Surely in God's infinite wisdom, there's a reason He created us with two ears and only one mouth. So, try to imagine for a moment how God feels when we are constantly doing all the talking, all the time.

God is the King of the Universe who does not tire or slumber, but we must learn how to attune our ears to Him. God speaks to us through scripture, prayer, the counsel of the saints, and other ways. But if we constantly do all the talking, it becomes impossible for us to listen. When God speaks to us, He will never contradict His word. God will not tell you to leave your spouse because you desire to be with someone else. At times, we might wrongly make God a cosmic scapegoat for our selfish desires, but that's not the focus here. We're talking about quieting ourselves before God and cutting out distractions to listen to the Almighty's guidance on the steps and changes needed for wholeness and healing in our lives.

That's why Step Eleven advocates integrating meditation into your daily regimen as you advance in your journey to recovery. Meditation serves as a tool that can give us inner peace. The gift God has given to each of us is the ability to talk with God but also to be silent in His presence. Contemplate how consistent meditative practices could enrich your recovery, and don't be afraid to try them.

Psalm 46:10 is all about practicing the stillness we all need in our society, which can positively impact us not only spiritually but in almost every area of our lives. In a noisy and strident world, hearing from God and being in God's presence is often a foreign concept. Look at practicing stillness almost as a cleansing of your mind and heart of the things that are troubling you in relationships at work, home, and elsewhere. At first, your mind will be racing with thoughts, but don't give up. Keep pressing in.

# DOING THE INNER WORK

Are you spending time with God on a daily basis? Are there distractions that are holding you back? List those on paper and name the challenges. How might you eliminate those distractions? Write that down as well under each distraction.

# PRAYER FOCUS

Dear God of Peace, steer me throughout my contemplative exercises. Allow me to discover Your essence, discernment, and tranquility in the calmness of my spirit. Instruct me on how to welcome serenity, not merely during periods of meditation but within every facet of my existence. So be it.

*Why do I meditate? Because I am a Christian. Therefore, every day in which I do not penetrate more deeply into the knowledge of God's Word in Holy Scripture is a lost day for me. I can only move forward with certainty upon the firm ground of the Word of God. – Deitrich Bonhoeffer*

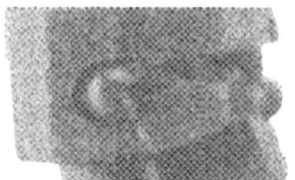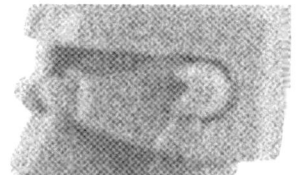

# DAY 37: UNDERSTANDING GOD'S WILL

*Trust in the LORD with all your heart and lean not on your own understanding; in all your ways submit to him, and he will make your paths straight.*
*— Proverbs 3:5-6*

## REFLECTION

As a pastor, I often encounter people longing to discern God's will for their lives and circumstances. In cases where there are no clear-cut answers, grasping and living by God's overarching will is crucial: to love God and to love our neighbors. When we take care of those things and seek after God in our daily lives, it's amazing how specific answers to prayers unfold before us. As we are on this recovery journey, we do not know the thousand next steps, but God will direct us to the right next step for our lives.

It is critical to be present in the here and now and not fear the future. If we are not present, we can miss the miraculous right in front of us. God has no desire to fool, trick, or take us off course. God wants to guide His children better than any earthly parent. God does not want to leave us in the dark but will light up the path along the journey.

In the Eleventh Step, our focus turns to understanding and acknowledging God's intentions. This phase surpasses merely choosing the right options; it involves aligning personal desires with a higher purpose. Reflect on how the concept of God's intentions has impacted your recovery process. How do you perceive it in your everyday existence? Ponder how pursuing God's guidance can help you to make decisions that you couldn't otherwise have made on your own.

# HEALING EXERCISE

Journal about moments when you felt you were in tune with God's will and reflect on the insights and growth from these experiences.

# PRAYER FOCUS

Dear God of all wisdom, guide me in understanding and following Your will. Help me to trust in Your divine guidance, even when the path is unclear. May my heart and actions reflect a deep desire to align with Your purpose for my life. Amen.

> *I believe that God has a plan and purpose not only for the human race but for my individual life.*
> *— Anne Graham Lotz*

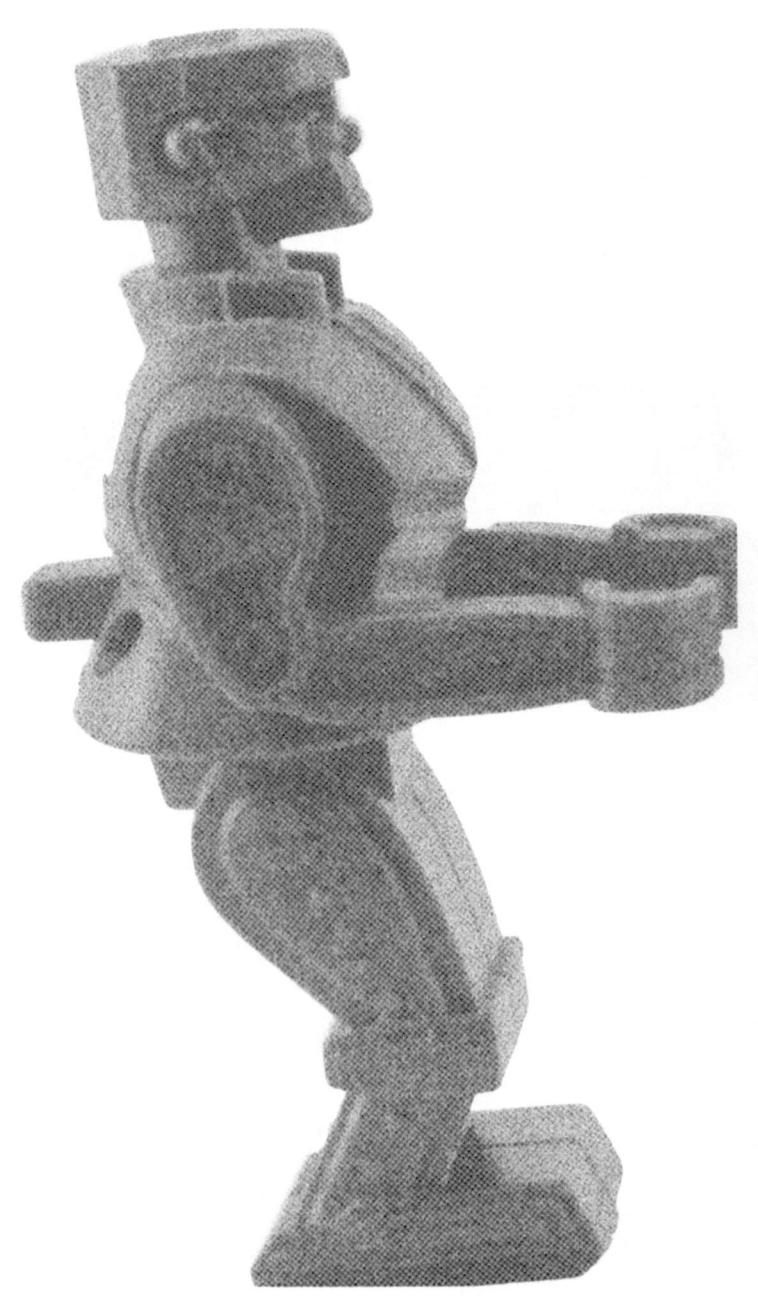

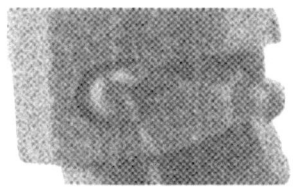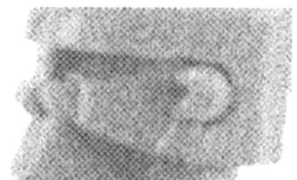

# DAY 38: DEFINING SPIRITUAL AWAKENING: STEP TWELVE

**STEP TWELVE: SHARE CHANGES**

## REFLECTION

One of the worst memories from Marine Corps Boot Camp in my mind was in the early morning when the Drill Instructors would wake us from a deep slumber after a long day. The norm was yelling and tossing trash cans—hardly a pleasant wake-up call. Some of us require our cup of coffee before engaging with others, while some are naturally more cheerful and prepared to tackle the day.

A spiritual awakening stirs us from our deep slumber of the former person we were like a newborn baby coming out of the womb, a new life after a long hibernation. Your spiritual awakening involves seeing yourself, others, the world, and, most of all, God for the first time in a new light. It also means getting to know a whole new world apart from mind-altering substances, hurts, hang-ups, addictions, compulsions, and behaviors. All of this takes time for us to adjust. But the new life you experience in Christ is and will be priceless.

Here in the twelfth step, you are urged to pause and contemplate the spiritual awakening that has been cultivated throughout your journey across these 12 Steps. Recovery for all of us is submitting our will to the care of God. As we invite God to take control of our lives and will, God will give us peace in difficult situations, heightened compassion toward others when we are in disagreements, and the ability to empathize with others who are going through challenges.

Pause for reflection upon how this transformation has shaped you. Reflect on those challenging instances alongside moments of victory. Each phase of doubt or introspection is crucial in leading you to this spiritual awakening.

This process involves recognizing every aspect of your journey, including hurdles cleared and triumphs won along the way. It entails acknowledging internal growth, which influences one's perception about life itself. Let this newfound awareness guide and motivate you while progressing further up this path of following Jesus.

As Ephesians 5:14 tells us, it's time to rise from slumber. We were once asleep at the wheel of our own lives. Now we are partnering with God in a life we never thought was possible. It is time to respond to that wake-up call. That call can come through a still, small voice or a thunderous one.

But the intent is the same: it's time to get out of bed and live the life Jesus has intended for you.

# PRAYER FOCUS

Almighty God, thank You that You are waking me up on a daily basis. As I wake up physically, allow me to be awake to Your Spirit. Guide me in every aspect of my life because my life is not my own but belongs to You. Help me to respond to You every day. In Jesus' name, Amen.

> *We are not human beings having a spiritual experience. We are spiritual beings having a human experience.* – *Pierre Teilhard de Chardin, S.J.*

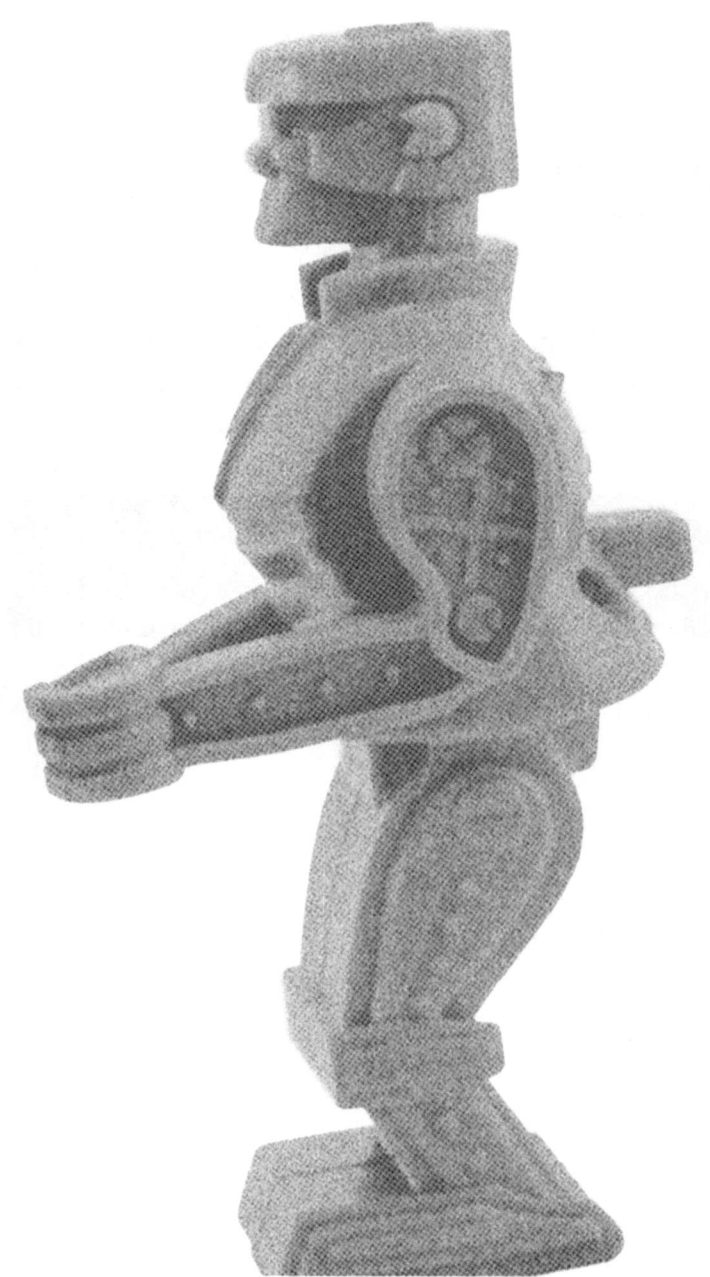

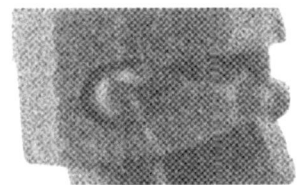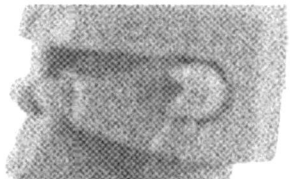

# DAY 39: SHARING YOUR EXPERIENCE

*Jesus did not let him, but said, "Go home to your own people and tell them how much the Lord has done for you, and how he has had mercy on you."*
*– Mark 5:19*

## REFLECTION

We can find great power in testimony and story. The early followers of Jesus understood this all too well. People experienced miracles in Jesus' earthly ministry. Though some were told not to say anything because His time had not yet come, they presumably shared anyway because they could not contain it. After the resurrection, the Gospel spread throughout the known world and caused a spiritual awakening. In the words of the Mystery of our Faith, Christ has died, Christ has risen, and Christ will come again.

Jesus' primary teaching mode was storytelling because He understood that stories carry images that are powerful for healing and transformation. God aims to transform our mess into our message, our test into our testimony. Our most significant failures and weaknesses can serve to glorify God and bring healing to others.

With that in mind, the Twelfth Step urges us to transcend personal development and share our experiences as a lighthouse of recovery for others. Our recovery story does not belong to us but belongs to God and God's people. Each and every experience adds to a story that can deeply resonate with others. Our journey embodies the real potential of persistence, faithfulness, and commitment to the 12 Steps, proving that transformation is possible.

At the same time, before sharing our story, we need to consider its possible ramifications on the minds of listeners. Many may find encouragement from hearing about how we navigated similar situations successfully, while others, still steeped in their own difficulties, may be triggered by some inadvertent remark. Let us therefore be sensitive to how specific aspects of our journey might resonate differently with our audiences. The narratives can offer realistic expectations in their recovery. Remember, it isn't always linear because the way will be dotted with trials and triumphs. Even our darkest periods contain a silver lining. They are all pathways toward healing and recovery through Jesus Christ. And Jesus wants to bring that same hope to others.

All that ripples outwards too! As storytellers share experiences openly and humbly, we acknowledge these tales aren't solely ours but that our sharing will become the testimony of others.

# DOING THE INNER WORK

As you think about sharing your story with someone else or with a group, what type of emotions come to your mind and heart? It's perfectly normal to experience a bit of fear and anxiety. Identify the negative and positive emotions that come to mind at the possibility of sharing those feelings with others.

## PRAYER FOCUS

Merciful God, empower me to share my recovery story and spiritual awakening. Let my words bring hope and encouragement to those who hear them, showing Your grace and love in my darkest of days. May my testimony be a light to others in their times of darkness. Amen.

> *When we can see God in our own struggles, we begin to see God in the struggles of others. This is the essence of what it means to share our story: to find God in all things, and to help others find God in their lives too. – Richard Rohr*

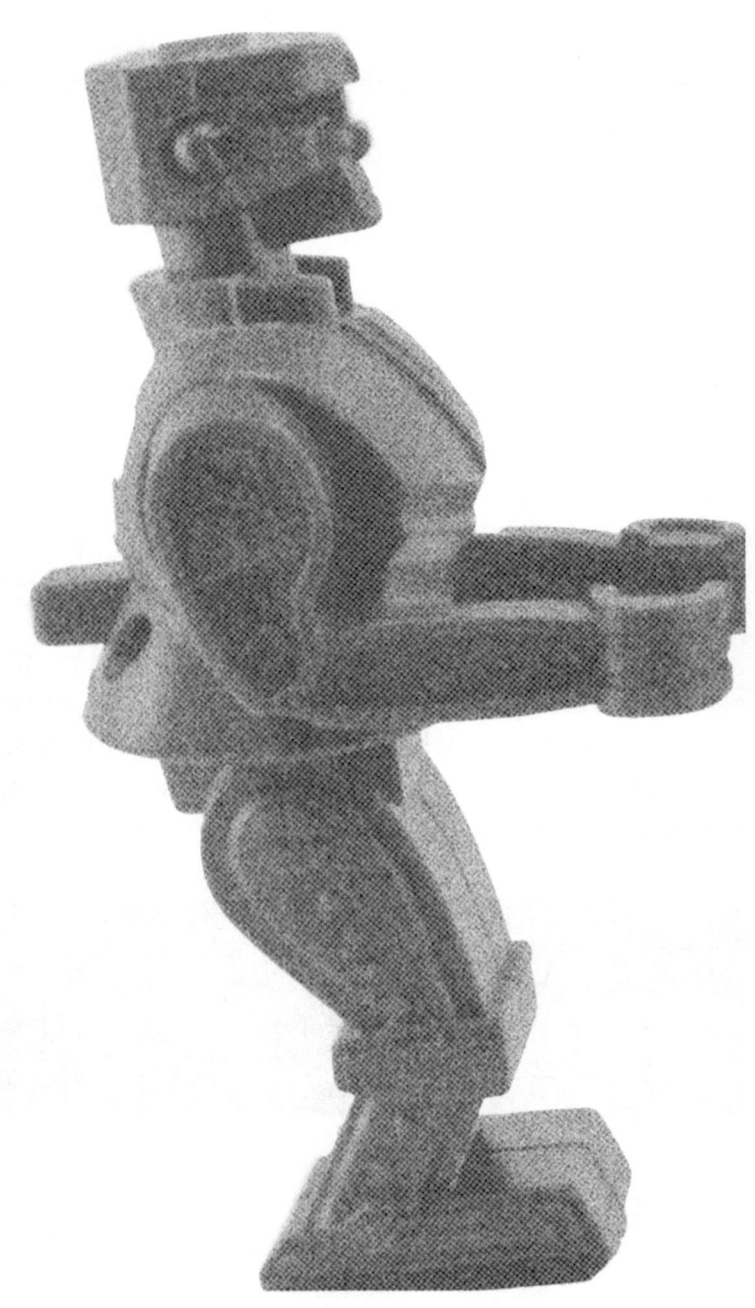

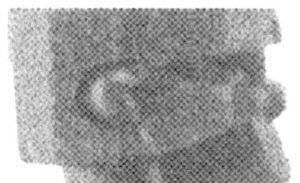
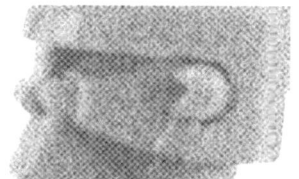

# DAY 40: RECOGNIZING THE CHANGE IN YOU

> *Therefore, if anyone is in Christ,*
> *the new creation has come.*
> *— 2 Corinthians 5:17*

## REFLECTION

If you've ever attempted to get in shape and lose weight, you understand how challenging the process can be. It's a journey filled with ups and downs, requiring commitment, perseverance, and lifestyle changes. From managing cravings to maintaining workout routines and staying motivated, it's a multifaceted endeavor that demands consistent effort and patience. Sometimes, instead of waiting for the scale to show progress, I prefer to go by how I feel, so I often put the scale away.

When we begin on that journey, it's slow, but after a while, those around us notice a difference and make comments—not those who live with you but those we see on occasion. When we recover our lives, the change may not be evident to us in the mirror, but others will take note. Sometimes, we are the last ones to recognize the transformation we have undergone. I want to encourage you to be kind to yourself on this life-long journey. You are changing and will be changed. It's a process. God is making you into a new creation. It is present and future change. The old has gone, and the new has come.

And so, as you near the completion of Step Twelve, it's crucial to take a moment and reflect on your remarkable journey. Dedicate some time to contemplate the scale and depth of your progress. Think of the hurdles and obstacles you have overcome with God's help. Think of the new insights gained that have redefined how you view yourself and your surroundings. You are not who you used to be. The person you are today will be changed for tomorrow. The steps are not a "one-and-done" type of deal but something we continue to go through our entire lives. They are not sequential. Different events and occasions will trigger certain emotions inside of you that need to be surrendered over to God. Don't let this alarm or discourage you. You are a new person. You are "becoming" new every day.

## HEALING EXERCISE

Have you ever pondered the idea of sharing your individual experiences with a person who could potentially gain from them? Could there perhaps be someone dealing with a similar circumstance or confronting a comparable hurdle that you once faced? By being transparent and conveying your story, you possess the capability to assist and steer others on their path. Think about which individuals in your life might find value in hearing about your personal journey and how it could positively influence their lives! Prayerfully begin making a list of people that God places on your heart to share with. After you have taken that time, ask for direction of the right place and time to do so.

# PRAYER FOCUS – THE SERENITY PRAYER

God, grant me the serenity to accept the things I cannot change, the courage to change the things I can, and the wisdom to know the difference. Living one day at a time, enjoying one moment at a time, accepting hardships as the pathway to peace, taking, as Jesus did, this sinful world as it is, not as I would have it, trusting that You will make all things right if I surrender to Your will, so that I may be reasonably happy in this life and supremely happy with You forever in the next. Amen.[1]

> *Spiritual formation, I have come to believe, is not about steps or stages on the way to perfection. It's about the movement from the mind to the heart through prayer in the presence of God.*
> *— Henri Nouwen*

---

1.      The Serenity Prayer is commonly attributed to Reinhold Niebuhr and is widely used in recovery and faith-based contexts. See *Hazelden Betty Ford Foundation*, "The Serenity Prayer," www.hazeldenbettyford.org/articles/the-serenity-prayer.

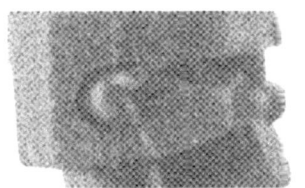
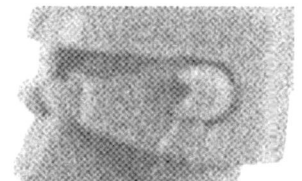

# DAY 41 (AND BEYOND): SHARING YOUR FIGHTING CHANCE

> *For we are God's masterpiece. He has created us anew*
> *in Christ Jesus, so we can do the good things*
> *he planned for us long ago.*
> *– Ephesians 2:10 (NLT)*

As we wrap up our 40-day journey through the 12 Steps, take a moment to recognize what God has done in you. I hope this journey has been a transformative experience, offering insights into self-awareness, healing, and spiritual growth.

Take time each day to ponder the lessons and insights you received from each step and revisit them often when overwhelming feelings resurface. Healing and recovery don't follow a straight path, and that's perfectly fine. These insights are not just confined to the past 40 days but serve as valuable tools for life. The journey has highlighted the importance of honesty, seeking guidance, making amends, and embracing spiritual awakening.

# NEXT STEPS FOR CONTINUED GROWTH

To continue your journey of growth and wisdom, consider the following steps:

1. **Regular Reflection**: Maintain the practice of self-reflection and inventory, which are vital for ongoing growth.

2. **Seek Community**: Engage with supportive communities, such as recovery groups or spiritual gatherings. Consider getting a sponsor or a spiritual mentor who can provide guidance, support, and accountability on your journey.

3. **Share Your Journey**: Your experiences can inspire and guide others. Consider sharing your story with those who might benefit from it.

4. **Deepen Your Spiritual Practice**: Continue exploring and deepening your spiritual practices, whether through prayer, meditation, or study.

5. **Stay Open to Learning**: Remain open to new insights and experiences contributing to your growth.

6. **Embrace Service**: Seek opportunities to give back and help others.

The 12-Step journey is an ongoing process of self-discovery and growth. Each day offers new opportunities to apply these principles.

# FINAL PRAYER FOCUS

Almighty God, thank You for accompanying me on this 40-day journey. As I continue forward, help me apply these lessons daily, guided by Your wisdom and love. Bless my efforts to seek community, find a sponsor or mentor, and share my story. May my path be one of continuous growth, service, and spiritual enrichment. Amen.

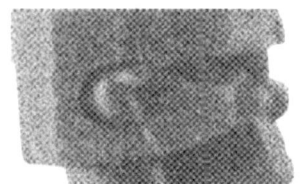

# BIBLIOGRAPHY

Alcoholics Anonymous. *Alcoholics Anonymous: The Story of How Thousands of Men and Women Have Recovered from Alcoholism.* 4th ed. New York: Alcoholics Anonymous

World Services, 2001.
Hazelden Betty Ford Foundation. "The Serenity Prayer." Hazelden Betty Ford Foundation, www.hazeldenbettyford.org/articles/the-serenity-prayer. Accessed 13 Nov. 2024.

Lucado, Max. *God Never Gives Up on You: What Jacob's Story Teaches Us About Grace, Mercy, and God's Relentless Love.* Nashville: Thomas Nelson, 2023.

Rohn, Jim. *The Art of Exceptional Living.* New York: Nightingale-Conant, 1993. Audio program.

Whelchel, Hugh. "What Is Shalom According to the Bible?" *Institute for Faith, Work, and Economics.* Accessed November 19, 2023. https://tifwe.org/what-is-shalom-according- to-the-bible/.

**SCAN HERE** to learn more about
Invite Ministries—created to invite people to a deeper
faith and living relationship with Jesus Christ